NATURAL RESOURCES

Forests

NATURAL RESOURCES

AGRICULTURE

ANIMALS

ENERGY

FORESTS

LANDS

MINERALS

PLANTS

WATER AND ATMOSPHERE

FORESTS

MORE THAN JUST TREES

Julie Kerr Casper, Ph.D.

CHELSEA HOUSE
PUBLISHERS
An imprint of Infobase Publishing

Forests

Copyright © 2007 by Julie Kerr Casper, Ph.D.

Chelsea House
An imprint of Infobase Publishing
132 West 31st Street
New York NY 10001

Library of Congress Cataloging-in-Publication Data
Casper, Julie Kerr.
    Forests : more than just trees / Julie Kerr Casper.
        p. cm.—(Natural resources)
    Includes bibliographical references.
    ISBN-13: 978–0–8160–6355–0 (hardcover)
    ISBN-10: 0–8160–6355–9 (hardcover)
  1. Forests and forestry—Juvenile literature. I. Title. II. Series.

    SD376.C375 2007
    333.75—dc22   2006100042

Chelsea House books are available at special discounts when purchased in bulk quantities for businesses, associations, institutions, or sales promotions. Please call our Special Sales Department in New York at (212) 967–8800 or (800) 322–8755.

You can find Chelsea House on the World Wide Web at http://www.chelseahouse.com

Text design by Erik Lindstrom
Cover design by Ben Peterson

Printed in the United States of America

Bang NMSG 10 9 8 7 6 5 4 3 2 1

This book is printed on acid-free paper.

All links and Web addresses were checked and verified to be correct at the time of publication. Because of the dynamic nature of the Web, some addresses and links may have changed since publication and may no longer be valid.

CONTENTS

Preface   vi

Acknowledgments   x

Introduction   xi

1   Concepts of Forest Resources   1

2   The Evolution of Forests   16

3   Renewable and Nonrenewable Resources   32

4   Development of Forest Resources   60

5   Uses of Forests and the Resulting Impacts   71

6   The Importance of Forest Resources   91

7   Management of Forest Resources
in a Rapidly Changing World   109

8   Conservation of Forests   130

9   Conclusion: The Future of the Forests   154

Appendix   165

Glossary   177

Further Reading   185

Index   188

PREFACE

NATURAL RESOURCES:
PRICELESS GIFTS FROM THE EARTH

Mankind did not weave the web of life.
We are but one strand in it. Whatever we
do to the web, we do to ourselves . . .
All things are bound together.

—Chief Seattle

The Earth has been blessed with an abundant supply of natural resources. Natural resources are those elements that exist on the planet for the use and benefit of all living things. Scientists commonly divide them down into distinct groups for the purposes of studying them. These groups include agricultural resources, plants, animals, energy sources, landscapes, forests, minerals, and water and atmospheric resources.

One thing we humans have learned is that many of the important resources we have come to depend on are not renewable. *Nonrenewable* means that once a resource is depleted it is gone forever. The fossil fuel that gasoline is produced from is an example of a nonrenewable resource. There is only a finite supply, and once it is used up, that is the end of it.

While living things such as animals are typically considered renewable resources, meaning they can potentially be replenished, animals hunted to extinction become nonrenewable resources. As we know from past evidence, the extinctions of the dinosaurs, the woolly mammoth, and the saber-toothed tiger were complete. Sometimes, extinctions like this may be caused by natural factors, such as climate change, drought, or flood, but many extinctions are caused by the activities of humans.

Overhunting caused the extinction of the passenger pigeon, which was once plentiful throughout North America. The bald eagle was hunted to the brink of extinction before it became a protected species, and African elephants are currently threatened with extinction because they are still being hunted for their ivory tusks. Overhunting is only one potential threat, though. Humans are also responsible for habitat loss. When humans change land use and convert an animal's habitat to a city, this destroys the animal's living space and food sources and promotes its endangerment.

Plants can also be endangered or become extinct. An important issue facing us today is the destruction of the Earth's tropical rain forests. Scientists believe there may be medicinal value in many plant species that have not been discovered yet. Therefore, destroying a plant species could be destroying a medical benefit for the future.

Because of human impact and influence all around the Earth, it is important to understand our natural resources, protect them, use them wisely, and plan for future generations. The environment—land, soil, water, plants, minerals, and animals—is a marvelously complex and dynamic system that often changes in ways too subtle to perceive. Today, we have enlarged our vision of the landscape with which we interact. Farmers manage larger units of land, which makes their job more complex. People travel greater distances more frequently. Even when they stay at home, they experience and affect a larger share of the world through electronic communications and economic activities—and natural resources have made these advancements possible.

The pace of change in our society has accelerated as well. New technologies are always being developed. Many people no longer spend all their time focused in one place or using things in traditional ways. People now move from one place to another and are constantly developing and using new and different resources.

A sustainable society requires a sustainable environment. Because of this, we must think of natural resources in new ways. Today, more than ever, we must dedicate our efforts to conserve the land. We still live in a beautiful, largely natural world, but that world is quickly changing. World population growth and our desire to live comfortably are exerting pressures on our soil, air, water, and other natural resources. As we destroy and fragment natural habitats, we continue to push nonhuman life into ever-smaller pockets. Today, we run the risk of those places becoming isolated islands on a domesticated landscape.

In order to be responsible caretakers of the planet, it is important to realize that we humans have a partnership with the Earth and the other life that shares the planet with us. This series presents a refreshing and informative way to view the Earth's natural resources. *Agriculture: The Food We Grow and Animals We Raise* looks at agricultural resources to see how responsible conservation, such as caring for the soil, will give us continued food to feed growing populations. *Plants: Life From the Earth* examines the multitude of plants that exist and the role they play in biodiversity. The use of plants in medicines and in other products that people use every day is also covered.

In *Animals: Creatures That Roam the Planet,* the series focuses on the diverse species of animals that live on the planet, including the important roles they have played in the advancement of civilization. This book in the series also looks at habitat destruction, exotic species, animals that are considered in danger of extinction, and how people can help to keep the environment intact.

Next, in *Energy: Powering the Past, Present, and Future*, the series explores the Earth's energy resources—such as renewable power from water, ocean energy, solar energy, wind energy, and biofuels; and non-renewable sources from oil shale, tar sands, and fossil fuels. In addition, the future of energy and high-tech inventions on the horizon are also explored.

In *Lands: Taming the Wilds,* the series addresses the land and how civilizations have been able to tame deserts, mountains, arctic regions, forests, wetlands, and floodplains. The effects that our actions can have on the landscape for years to come are also explored. In *Forests: More Than Just Trees,* the series examines the Earth's forested areas and how unique and important these areas are to medicine, construction, recreation, and commercial products. The effects of deforestation, pest outbreaks, and wildfires—and how these can impact people for generations to come—are also addressed.

In *Minerals: Gifts From the Earth*, the bounty of minerals in the Earth and the discoveries scientists have made about them are examined. Moreover, this book in the series gives an overview of the critical part minerals play in many common activities and how they affect our lives every day.

Finally, in *Water and Atmosphere: The Lifeblood of Natural Systems*, the series looks at water and atmospheric resources to find out just how these resources are the lifeblood of the natural system—from drinking water, food production, and nutrient storage to recreational values. Drought, sea-level rise, soil management, coastal development, the effects of air and water pollution, and deep-sea exploration and what it holds for the future are also explored.

The reader will learn the wisdom of recycling, reducing, and reusing our natural resources, as well as discover many simple things that can be done to protect the environment. Practical approaches such as not leaving the water running while brushing your teeth, turning the lights off when leaving a room, using reusable cloth bags to transport groceries, building a backyard wildlife refuge, planting a tree, forming a carpool, or starting a local neighborhood recycling program are all explored.

Everybody is somebody's neighbor, and shared responsibility is the key to a healthy environment. The cheapest—and most effective—conservation comes from working with nature. This series presents things that people can do for the environment now and the important role we all can play for the future. As a wise Native-American saying goes, "We do not inherit the Earth from our ancestors—we borrow it from our children."

ACKNOWLEDGMENTS

I would sincerely like to thank the army of dedicated people who work for the U.S. Forest Service and strive to ensure the health, productivity, and natural beauty of America's forests. I would also like to recognize all those people who are actively involved in conservation and research organizations for the hard work they do to promote and maintain a sustainable environment (see Conservation Organizations in the Glossary). Many thanks to Karl Lehman of lostworldarts.com for the beautiful rain forest flower photography. The focus of Lehmann's photography is dedicated toward the amazing heritage of biodiversity and human cultures in the hope that raising awareness will inspire people to appreciate how valuable and irreplaceable they are. In addition, I would like to express my immense gratitude to Rhett Butler of WildMadagascar.org and Mongabay.com for his breathtaking photography throughout the Earth's multitude of diverse rain forest environments. Butler's Mongabay.com seeks to raise interest in, and appreciation of, wild lands and wildlife, while examining the impact of emerging local and global trends in technology, economics, and finance on conservation and development. He is currently involved in critical rain forest projects.

INTRODUCTION

Forests are some of the richest, most diverse areas in the world. Over millions of years, they have developed in the various environments on Earth. Forests are large areas that are not only covered with trees but also plants, grasses, and flowers. They are inhabited by a myriad of different life-forms. Forests are essential to life on Earth—they help regulate the Earth's atmosphere, providing enough oxygen for humans and other organisms to breathe. Forests also provide many important services, such as providing habitats for millions of plants and animals. In fact, more than half of all known species are found in the world's rain forests.

Throughout history, people have utilized the unique resources of the forests for shelter, for food (such as fruit), and for wood to use in building and providing energy (fuel). Forest plants also provide food, dyes, medicines, and many other products that people use, and rely on, every day.

Unfortunately, with the Earth's growing population and the impacts of modernization, forests are in danger of being destroyed—being cut down or burned—at rapid rates. If forests are removed, scientists believe the effects would be far-reaching; it would change the composition of the Earth's atmosphere, making the environment very different from what it is today.

This volume in the Natural Resources series focuses on the many aspects that make forests such a valuable natural resource. Chapter 1 discusses the factors that control where forests grow, the forest environment, the types of forests, and their geographical distribution.

Chapter 2 looks at the evolution of forests, their biodiversity, succession, and the processes that control them.

Chapter 3 examines the various resources provided by forests, both renewable and nonrenewable. It focuses on wildlife, indigenous peoples, the importance and role of soil, and the multitude of botanical resources stored in forests.

Chapter 4 explores the development and processes of forests, such as the water cycle, photosynthesis, and evapotranspiration. It also looks at adaptations required by plants and animals in order to survive in forest environments, as well as the critical functions of food chains.

Chapter 5 examines the many uses of the forest and forest products. It looks at current impacts of human activity on forests, such as logging, burning, clearing, fire, overexploitation, habitat loss and degradation, pollution, and deforestation.

Chapter 6 discusses the importance of forests and the goods and services they provide to society every day, such as medicines, wildlife, timber and nontimber products, recreation, and energy resources.

Chapter 7 illustrates how this important resource is being managed today in a rapidly changing world. It discusses the consequences of overuse, including overhunting, overfishing, and overgrazing; timber management; watershed management; insect and disease management; and fire management; it also discusses the current technologies that are used today to manage forests in a safe and productive way in order to support sustainable forestry.

Chapter 8 presents the most crucial conservation issues that managers face today and how they are being dealt with. This chapter looks at endangered species; preservation measures; the effects of pollution; genetically engineered trees; protective initiatives; the practice of shifting cultivation; and maintaining the fragile, delicate balance in these areas on a global scale. It also looks at backyard conservation and the critical role of public awareness and education.

Finally, Chapter 9 covers future issues and scientific discoveries that illustrate how forests improve our standard of living. It also examines the concept of sustainable forestry; preservation of the rain forests; the importance of recycling, reducing, and reusing; and the simple things everyone can do to help maintain healthy forest ecosystems all over the world.

CONCEPTS OF FOREST RESOURCES

Forests are usually defined as land areas dominated by trees where the tree **canopy** covers at least 10% of the ground area. Some people may think forests merely consist of large groups of trees; but in reality, a forest is much more than that. Before people began clearing forests for agriculture, forests covered about 20% more land than they do now—equivalent to roughly half of the Earth's landmass.

Since 1980, forested area has decreased by 10% in developing countries. In tropical regions, **deforestation** is estimated to exceed 50,193 square miles (130,000 square kilometers) per year. In Northern Hemisphere countries, forested area is either holding steady or increasing. In the United States and countries of Western Europe, where nearly all forests are managed to some degree, forested area has increased because previously deforested areas have been replanted or allowed to regenerate on their own. Forest environments abound with a huge variety of plants, shrubs, flowers, animals, insects, and birds. All of these elements working and living together create a successful forest **ecosystem**.

Today, about 30% of the Earth's land areas are covered in forests. There are five major types of forests: **boreal**, **temperate deciduous**, **temperate coniferous**, **temperate rain forests**, and **tropical rain forests**. This chapter looks at the various factors that control where trees grow, characteristics of the forest environment, the different types of forests and what makes them unique, and the geographical distribution of the world's forests.

FACTORS THAT CONTROL WHERE FORESTS GROW

Anywhere on the Earth's surface where there is warmth, light, air, mineral **nutrients** in the soil, and water, plants (including trees) can survive. The various geographical areas where plants can survive are called **habitats**. The conditions that affect plant growth in a habitat are physical, such as climate and geography, or biotic (i.e., the effects of plants on each other), as well as the effects of humans and animals on plants.

Climatic factors that affect plant diversity include temperature, precipitation, **humidity** (moisture in the air), wind patterns, and the availability of light. Geographic factors include topography, soil type, and drainage.

Temperature ranges and humidity directly affect what can grow successfully. For example, rain forest vegetation that demands a hot, humid environment could not grow in Arctic regions because it is too cold and dry. Temperature extremes on a daily basis also play a significant role in the composition of native vegetation. Precipitation refers to all water that reaches the Earth's surface (such as snow, rain, and frost). The average annual rainfall of an area and the way it is distributed throughout the year influences many plants. For example, areas that are warm and moist in the summer will support different vegetation than hot, dry areas. Many plants require certain temperatures at specific times in order to successfully complete their life cycles. Some plants require different daily periods of light in order to survive. Light intensity is a critical factor in the process of **photosynthesis**. Soil properties, such as pH (acidity or alkalinity), depth, and fertility are critical in determining what can grow.

The land's surface is also important in determining what types of plants can grow. For example, slopes support different types of vegetation than valley bottoms, and slopes with different aspects—such as north facing or south facing—will have different types or densities of plant life.

There are thousands of different habitats in the world. They are often referred to by their dominant conditions, such as rain forest, temperate forest, boreal forest, tundra, alpine, wetland, coastal, savanna/grassland, and desert. The types of plants that grow in them further characterize habitats.

Within each habitat, every plant has its own **niche**. Each niche is slightly different. Generally, two different types of plants cannot survive in the same niche. If two types of plants compete for the same light, water, space, and nutrients, one will become dominant and the other will die off. Ecology is the science that looks at ways in which plants affect their environment and are affected by it.

Plant **biodiversity** is when an ecosystem in one area has an abundance of different plant **species**. These species must range from grasses to shrubs and flowers to large trees to be a biodiverse ecosystem. When an ecosystem is biodiverse, it allows for many more species to live and thrive there. If an invasive species is introduced into an ecosystem, it could harm the biodiversity of the existing ecosystem. Invasive species push out species that are native to the area, because native species often have less tolerance to change in an existing habitat than an invasive species does. The invasive species also lacks the natural **predators** and controls that govern the native species. Subsequent loss in biodiversity—when the invasive plant destroys the native ones—can affect everything from animal diversity to climatic changes.

THE FOREST BIOME

Present-day forest **biomes**—biological communities that are dominated by trees and other woody vegetation—can be classified into specific biomes by certain characteristics, especially their seasonality

Giant sequoias are found in northern California. These trees can grow as tall as a 38-story building. *(Photo courtesy National Park Service)*

(precipitation, temperature, humidity, and length of growing season). Most forest trees grow to be about 20 to 30 feet (6 to 9 meters) tall. In healthy living conditions, many can live as long as 200 years. There are some exceptions, however. The sequoia trees in California reach heights of over 360 feet (110 m). The wood from one of those trees could be used to build 50 houses. Sequoias can live more than 3,000 years. The bristlecone pine can live for more than 4,500 years.

In most forests, the sunlight filtering down to the forest floor appears dim because of the forest canopy above. The canopy is a layer of leaves and branches high above the ground. This layer is thick enough to keep the Sun's heat out of the forest. The canopy also keeps much of the forest's water from escaping into the air. By keeping the forest shady and moist, the canopy makes the climatic environment perfect for other plants to grow, which is why more than 1,000 species of plants can live in a single forest environment.

Forests, wooded areas, and scattered trees have provided food, fuel, medicines, filtered water, shelter, and building materials throughout time. As countries with sizable forest resources develop, they tend to rely heavily on **timber** production over other services provided by forests. More than half of the world's remaining forests lie in developing countries, which places stress on the forest resources.

In these countries, millions of people still depend on forests for food (such as fruit, nuts, mushrooms, and game), building and household materials (such as timber, vines, and bamboo), and fodder to feed their livestock. In addition, traditional goods—such as wood fuels and medicines—still serve as the basis for livelihoods for many rural populations. Managing these forest resources in developing countries is critical in order to maintain the health and diversity of forest ecosystems.

There are three broad groups of forests classed according to latitude: boreal (also called **taiga**), temperate, and **tropical forests**. Within each major group, a variety of forest types occur.

TYPES OF FORESTS

In addition to geographic latitude, a forest's seasonal behavior characterizes which type of forest environment it is classified as—either a boreal, temperate, or tropical environment.

Forests of the World

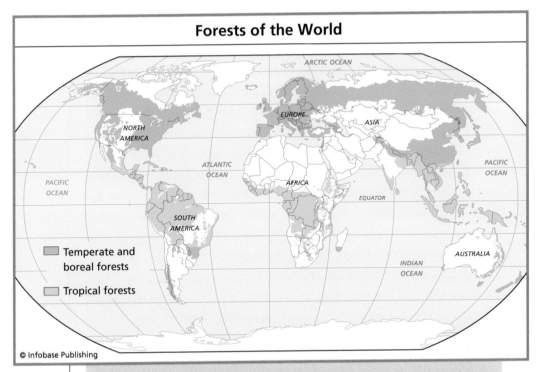

Forests occupy about one-third of the Earth's land areas. The tropical forests are located along the equatorial regions of the Earth, between the Tropic of Cancer and the Tropic of Capricorn. Most of the temperate and boreal forests are found in the Northern Hemisphere, because the Southern Hemisphere lacks the landmasses necessary for these forests to survive.

Boreal Forests

The term *boreal* means "northern." Boreal forests—also referred to as *taiga* (a Russian word)—are only present in the Northern Hemisphere; the Southern Hemisphere has very little land at the typical boreal forest latitudes (50°–60°). These areas represent the northernmost reaches where tree species can survive. The boreal region encircles the Earth across the Northern Hemisphere through Canada, Russia, Scandinavia, and Alaska. It represents the world's largest terrestrial biome. The main plant life of this northern sub-Arctic and humid region consists of coniferous larches, spruces, pines, and firs, which are adapted to the cold climate. Conifers keep their needles year-round. Because of this, most conifers are always green—which is why they are also referred to as **evergreens**. Evergreens are different from deciduous trees, such as oak, maple, and elm. The leaves of deciduous trees fall off every autumn, and new leaves grow every spring. Some **broadleaf** trees also occur—namely birches, aspens, and willows. Temperatures in this region remain very low, and most of the precipitation is in the form of snow—16 to 39 inches (40 to 100 centimeters) each year.

The boreal forest soil tends to be thin, nutrient-poor, and acidic, due to the vegetation. When needles that have fallen from conifers decompose, they have a special adaptation. They secrete an acid that helps prevent plants other than conifers from growing. Because the forest's canopy only permits a small amount of light through it, the forest understory is very limited. The ecosystem of the boreal region is a swath of conifer and deciduous trees that acts as part of the largest source and filter of freshwater on the planet.

The boreal forest in Canada is the largest contiguous (connected) intact forest left on Earth; it covers 35% of the country's landmass spreading over areas from north of Newfoundland to the Yukon. These northern forests also serve as the breeding grounds for more than half of Canada's bird population. Birds, such as the Siberian thrush, White's thrush, and dark-throated thrush, migrate to this habitat to take advantage of the long summer days and abundant insect food during that season. The area also provides natural habitat for the golden eagle, raven, crossbill, and rough-legged buzzard.

The boreal forests also support the world's largest caribou herd; the second-largest wolf population; and polar, black, and grizzly bears. They also provide homes for woodpeckers, hawks, moose, weasels (wolverines), lynxes, foxes, and deer.

Temperate Forests

The Earth's temperate forests are located midway between the **tropics** and the poles. The temperate climate is moderate—neither extremely hot nor extremely cold. The summers can feel hot and dry, but these forests never get so harsh that the soil dries up or the plants die. Likewise, the winters may see a lot of snow, but winters are not as severe

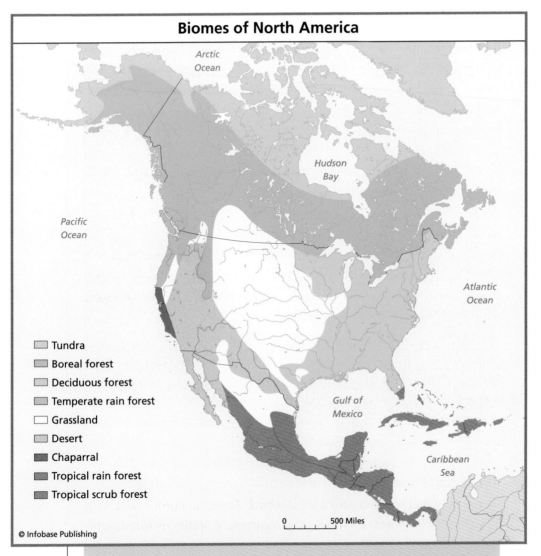

Biomes of North America

Arctic
Ocean

Hudson
Bay

Pacific
Ocean

Atlantic
Ocean

☐ Tundra
☐ Boreal forest
☐ Deciduous forest
☐ Temperate rain forest
☐ Grassland
☐ Desert
☐ Chaparral
☐ Tropical rain forest
☐ Tropical scrub forest

Gulf of
Mexico

Caribbean
Sea

0 ____ 500 Miles

© Infobase Publishing

The biomes of North America. This map illustrates the diverse range of forest types that exist, ranging from boreal forest to tropical rain forest environments.

as in the boreal forests. Temperate forests can be coniferous, deciduous, or contain mixed vegetation, depending on where they lay geographically and on the local climate.

Temperate coniferous forests in North America provide many recreational opportunities, such as hiking, fishing, and camping. This is Wasatch National Forest, located in northern Utah, at an elevation of approximately 9,000 feet (2,743 m). *(Photo courtesy Nature's Images)*

Temperate coniferous forests

These grow in the lower latitudes of North America, Europe, and Asia, as well as in the high elevations of mountains. Coniferous forests consist mostly of conifers—trees that grow needles instead of leaves, and cones instead of flowers. Conifers are evergreens, keeping their color all year. These special **adaptations** help conifers survive in areas that are very cold and very dry. This is because conifers' waxy needles do not lose as much moisture as the leaves of other trees do.

Precipitation in coniferous forests varies from 12 to 35 inches (30 to 90 cm) each year, with some forests receiving up to 79 inches (200 cm) a year. The forest's geographic location determines how much rainfall it receives.

These forest regions have cold, long, snowy winters; warm, humid summers; well-defined seasons; and at least four to six frost-free months. Many species of trees inhabit these forests, including cedar, cypress, Douglas fir, juniper, pine, and spruce. The understory also contains a wide variety of herbaceous and shrub species. These forests are common in the coastal areas of regions that have mild winters and heavy rainfall; they are also found inland in drier climates or mountain areas.

Forest variations are dependent on the amount of rainfall that the area receives:

- Moist conifer and evergreen broad-leaved forests—these have wet winters and dry summers. Rainfall is concentrated in the winter months, and the winters are relatively mild.
- Dry conifer forests—these dominate the higher elevation zones and have low amounts of precipitation.
- Mediterranean forests—here precipitation is concentrated in the winter, and these areas receive less than 39 inches (100 cm) of precipitation per year.
- Temperate coniferous—these have mild winters and high annual precipitation of more than 79 inches (200 cm).

Temperate deciduous forests

These forests can be found in the eastern portion of the United States and Canada, most of Europe, and parts of China and Japan. The temperate deciduous forest biome is constantly changing—it has four distinct seasons: spring, summer, autumn, and winter. Winters are cold and summers are warm. Temperatures in these forests range from –20°F to 86°F (–30°C to 30°C). Annual precipitation (30 to 59 inches or 75 to 150 cm) is distributed evenly throughout the year. Because the soil is very fertile—enriched with decaying ground **litter**—and **hardwood** trees are good for building, this biome contains some of the world's largest cities, which utilize the wood for construction.

In the winter, less water is available for trees to take in through their roots, because much of the water in the ground is frozen. Since trees lose water through their leaves, losing leaves is a way for a tree to conserve water. The broad, flat leaves of deciduous trees lose water quickly. Therefore, the leaves of deciduous trees change color and fall off in the autumn and grow back in the spring after being dormant all winter. They also have thick bark to protect them from the cold weather. Trees grow during the spring and summer growing season.

According to New Hampshire Public Television (NHPTV), temperate deciduous forests have a great variety of plant species. Most have three levels of plants. The forest floor is usually inhabited by lichen, moss, ferns, wildflowers, and other small plants. Shrubs fill in the middle level; and hardwood trees (maple, oak, birch, sweet gum, beech, hickory, hemlock, cottonwood, elm, willow, and magnolia) make up the top level.

The animals that live in these forests must be able to adapt to the changing seasons. Some animals in this biome migrate or hibernate in the winter. Several species, such as squirrels, skunks, deer, bobcats, mountain lions, birds, rabbits, black bears, foxes, and timber wolves inhabit these forests.

Tropical Forests

Rain forests are the most lush and fertile places on Earth. They are home to an amazing variety of plant and animal life, supporting the Earth's most diverse ecosystems. A rain forest is an area of dense tropical forest, where the temperature and rainfall are high and steady all year long. Temperatures range from 68°F to 77°F (20°C to 25°C), keeping the area warm and frost-free all year. Rainfall averages 79 to 394 inches (200 to 1,000 cm) a year. A rain forest, when seen from above, looks like a thick sea of green because its vegetation is so dense.

Rain forests have more wildlife than any other habitat. For example, scientists believe that 3 acres of the South American rain forest contains up to 42,000 species of insects, 750 species of trees, 1,500 other plant species, and a huge population of birds and other animals. Trees range in height from 165 to 350 feet (50 to 108 m).

Rain forests occur in South America, Africa, and Asia. Most are between the Tropic of Cancer (23.5° N latitude) north of the equator, and the Tropic of Capricorn (23.5° S latitude) south of the equator. Rain forests require at least 79 inches (200 cm) of rain spread throughout the year. It is the extreme warmth and humidity that make the vegetation flourish. There are two types of rain forests: tropical and temperate.

Tropical rain forests

These forests are found closer to the equator where it is warm. Over half of all tropical rain forests occur in South America. The largest area of rain forest is in Brazil, which represents one-third of all the world's tropical rain forests. The Amazon is the world's largest single tropical rain forest. It covers a region in South America that is nearly as large as the continental United States.

The tropical rain forest is a hot, moist biome where it rains all year long. It does not have distinct seasons; its plants are green throughout the year. Instead of being defined by temperature, seasons in the tropics are determined by the amount of rainfall.

The tropical rain forest is known for its dense canopies of vegetation that form four different levels: ground, low forest, mid-forest, and the canopy. Each level of the forest has its own characteristic vegetation and animal life. Very little sunlight reaches the ground. Since plants cannot grow without sunlight, most of the forest floor has little vegetation, except along the riverbanks. In order to be competitive, plants grow tall without growing as wide as trees in moderate climates.

The bottom layer—or floor—of the rain forest is covered with wet leaves and leaf litter. This material decomposes rapidly in the wet, warm conditions and sends nutrients back into the soil. The hot, moist atmosphere and all the dead plant material also create the perfect conditions in which bacteria and other microorganisms can thrive.

The forest floor is inhabited by scores of creatures. Most of the organisms that live on the ground are **decomposers**, tiny creatures that

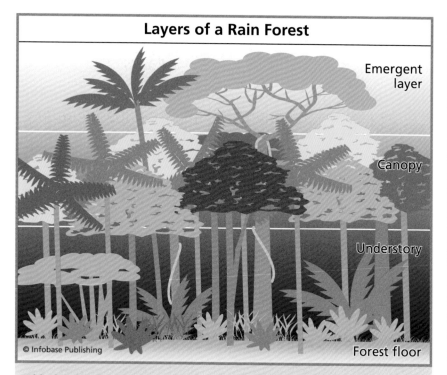

Layers of a Rain Forest

Emergent layer

Canopy

Understory

© Infobase Publishing

Forest floor

This drawing illustrates the structure of a rain forest and its four distinct layers: the forest floor, the understory, the canopy, and the emergent layer. Each layer hosts its own ecosystem with specific plants and animals.

feed on dead plant and animal materials. They include a variety of insects, **fungi**, and bacteria. These organisms are so abundant that dead leaves and small animals rarely remain on the ground for more than a day before they are consumed.

Larger creatures also inhabit the forest floor. Elephants, hippopotamuses, and water buffalo live on the floor of the African and Asian rain forests. Armadillos, coatimundis, and several tropical rodents occupy the ground level of the Amazon.

Located above the ground is the low-level forest. This layer is inhabited by colonies of insects that are found nowhere else on Earth. Most plants in the low-level forest have wide, leathery leaves. The wide leaves help the plants absorb what little light there is from the dim forest interior.

Above the plants of the low-level forest, the mid-level has slender tree trunks that stretch toward the sky. They are covered with moss and **lichens** and provide habitat for tropical insects. Many creatures that live in this level are so well **camouflaged** that they are almost invisible. Most of the tropical birds—like macaws—have bright blue, yellow, green, and red feathers, allowing them to blend in with the forest's flowers and leaves. The middle layer—or understory—is made up of vines, smaller trees, ferns, and palms.

Above the open spaces of the mid-level forest is the canopy—the topmost level of a tropical rain forest. The top layer—or canopy—contains giant trees that grow to heights of 250 feet (75 m) or more. This layer of vegetation prevents much of the sunlight from reaching the ground. Thick, woody vines are also found in the canopy, where they climb the trees to reach for sunlight.

The forest canopy differs from the dark forest interior. Besides receiving more sunlight, the top of the forest also receives more moisture than the forest floor. Some of the rain that falls on a tropical forest never reaches the ground, because the leaves and branches of the canopy trees absorb it.

In the canopy, there is sunlight, wind, rain, and variations in temperature. Flowers and fruits are found here and so are the animals that eat them, such as insects and tree frogs. A few trees are even taller and stick up above the canopy. This is referred to as the **emergent layer**.

Temperate rain forests

These forests are found near the cooler coastal areas further north or south of the equator. They are also found along some coasts in temperate zones. The largest temperate rain forests are found on the Pacific Coast of North America. They stretch from Oregon to Alaska for 1,200 miles (1,930 km). Smaller temperate rain forests can be found on the southeast of Chile in South America. There are a few other coastal strips with temperate rain forests, including small areas in the United Kingdom, Norway, Japan, New Zealand, and southern Australia.

Comparison of Tropical and Temperate Rain Forests

	Tropical	Temperate
Temperatures	Warm	Cool
Number of tree species	Hundreds	Few (10–20)
Types of leaves	Broadleaf	Needles
Age of trees	50–100 years	500–1,000 years
Epiphytes (Plants that grow on other plants)	Diverse, including orchids and bromeliads	Mostly mosses and ferns
Decomposition rate	Rapid	Slow

(Source: Missouri Botanical Garden)

Temperate rain forests show seasonal variation between summer and winter temperatures. The cool winters limit the number and kinds of life-forms that live there. Compared to the tropical rain forest, the temperate rain forest has a less complex ecology. According to the David Suzuki Foundation, they represent some of the rarest ecosystems in the world, and originally comprised less than 0.02% of the Earth's land surface. Approximately half of all original temperate forests have been logged. Coastal temperate rain forests have four defining characteristics: (1) a proximity to oceans, (2) presence of coastal mountains, (3) cooler summer temperatures, and (4) high rainfall levels.

Tropical and temperate rain forests also share certain characteristics. For example, most trees flare at the base. Vegetation is dense, tall, and very green, and rain falls regularly throughout the year. Both types of rain forests are rich in plant and animal species, although the diversity is greater in the tropical rain forest. The table above compares the characteristics of the two types of rain forests.

THE EVOLUTION OF FORESTS

Even though forests may seem permanent and unchanging over time, they are, in fact, always changing. Several things can affect a forest's stability—storms, wildfires, climate cycles, pest and disease cycles, and even the movement of entire continents. But an even bigger impact on forests is the recent influence of humans. Human activity has caused rapid change in a short time span, with greater consequences than other cataclysmic events have throughout geologic time. This chapter looks at the change in forests over time, how they adapt in order to survive, how they develop and mature, the impact of human civilizations on forest resources over time, and the importance of biodiversity.

FORESTS OVER TIME

The continents on the Earth have not always been in the same geographical locations they are in today. At one point in geologic time, the world was made up of a single continent, called Pangaea. This

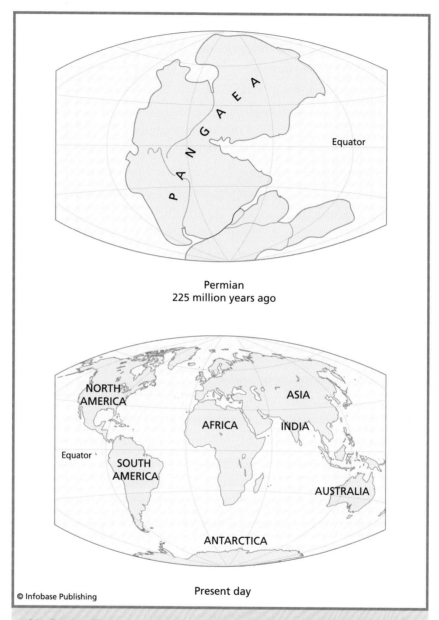

Permian
225 million years ago

NORTH
AMERICA

ASIA

AFRICA   INDIA

Equator

SOUTH
AMERICA

AUSTRALIA

ANTARCTICA

© Infobase Publishing

Present day

This diagram illustrates what the "supercontinent" Pangaea looked like millions of years ago. Over geologic time, the different continents broke apart and drifted over the Earth into the present-day configuration of continents. Scientists have been able to put this puzzle together by studying fossil remains of ancient tropical forests in areas that today are too cold or dry to support those types of forests.

"supercontinent" eventually separated and drifted apart, forming the seven different continents that exist today.

Several factors determine what types of forests can successfully grow in a specific location. Temperature, rainfall, amount of sunlight, wind, soil type, the interaction of other plants as well as animals, and the effects of urbanization all play a critical role in determining which types of trees will be successful. This also explains why geologists and paleontologists have discovered remains of massive prehistoric forests in areas that are too cold, hot, or dry today to support forests—such as in Saudi Arabia.

About 415 million years ago (mya), during the Silurian period, ancient plants and animals began to occupy the land. In the Middle Devonian, true roots developed and soils began to form. With this, plants developed an even more complex vascular system, which provided them more stability so they could grow to greater heights. These developments created all the basic conditions needed for trees to grow, allowing forests to begin spreading over the land during the Late Devonian. Scientists have determined that the wood of these forests was similar to the conifers of today.

Over the millions of years that followed, trees developed and adapted to their new habitat. Giant horsetails, club mosses, and ferns that stood up to 40 feet (12 m) tall dominated the first forests. The environment was largely swampy and primeval.

Life on Earth continued to evolve, and by the late Paleozoic (260 mya), **gymnosperms** (seed-producing plants) appeared. Plants had fern-like fronds and did not reproduce with spores, but with real seeds and pollen grains. During the Carboniferous period, roughly 320 mya, plants became more complex. It was during this time that many of the large coal formations on Earth were formed. Coal formed in areas that were swampy. Dying trees collected in bogs and then became buried and compacted over geologic time, eventually transforming into thick coal beds. During the Carboniferous, large areas of Europe and North America were situated in equatorial positions where extensive swamp forests existed.

At the end of the Permian (250 mya), roughly 95% of all plant and animal species became extinct. This represents the largest mass

This illustration depicts what the first prehistoric forests may have looked like—much different than forests on Earth today.

extinction in the Earth's history. Scientists today still have not come to a single conclusion as to the exact cause.

By the Triassic period (250–205 mya), gymnosperms dominated the Earth's forests. In the Cretaceous period (135–66 mya), the first flowering plants (angiosperms) appeared. They evolved together with mammals, birds, and insects. Angiosperms dominated the Earth's surface by the end of this period. Like today, different trees grew in different places, as determined by local geography and climate.

Then, during the Pleistocene ice ages (beginning 100,000 years ago), the Earth's surface—which had been dominated by tropical forests for millions of years—changed, and temperate forests spread in the Northern Hemisphere. Every 100,000 years or so, an ice age occurs. The climate gets colder everywhere, and the ice sheets that cover the poles spread out, engulfing vast areas of land and sea. The last ice age ended about 10,000 years ago. At its peak, ice sheets spread into the United States and northern Europe. The temperate forests were wiped from these regions by the ice, but in North America, most of the temperate plant species survived by migrating south to warmer climates. Once the ice sheets retreated, the temperate forests migrated north again. In Europe, however, the mountainous areas of the Alps and Pyrenees kept the temperate forests from being able to migrate south. Because of this, many European plant species were wiped out, which is why they have fewer species of temperate forest plants than North America today.

ADAPTATIONS—MECHANISMS FOR SURVIVAL

Being able to adapt to current environmental conditions is important in order for forests to survive over time. If forest stands do not adapt, they die off. Several survival mechanisms have evolved over geologic

Prehistoric Forests and Amber

The gem known as amber, made famous in the movie *Jurassic Park*, is actually a by-product of trees—specifically, it is a **resin**. Like tree sap today, it was a sticky, viscous fluid. It often covered and trapped small animals, insects, leaves, and stems that came in contact with it. Often, the value of amber as a commercial gemstone in today's market is increased if it does contain inclusions such as these. Amber is also a useful tool to help scientists study the past. Amber was a commodity often traded on ancient trade routes. If scientists can identify the geographic source of a particular piece of amber, it allows archaeologists to understand past civilizations—much like putting the pieces of a puzzle together.

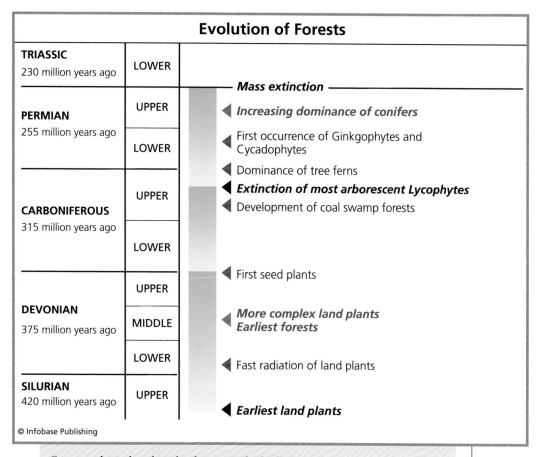

Evolution of Forests

TRIASSIC 230 million years ago	LOWER	
PERMIAN 255 million years ago	UPPER	
	LOWER	
CARBONIFEROUS 315 million years ago	UPPER	
	LOWER	
DEVONIAN 375 million years ago	UPPER	
	MIDDLE	
	LOWER	
SILURIAN 420 million years ago	UPPER	

———— *Mass extinction* ————

◀ *Increasing dominance of conifers*

◀ First occurrence of Ginkgophytes and Cycadophytes

◀ Dominance of tree ferns

◀ *Extinction of most arborescent Lycophytes*

◀ Development of coal swamp forests

◀ First seed plants

◀ *More complex land plants*
Earliest forests

◀ Fast radiation of land plants

◀ *Earliest land plants*

© Infobase Publishing

Forests adapted and evolved over geologic time.

time to ensure a forest's long-term existence. At the Earth's beginning, living things could not survive on Earth because the atmosphere contained poisonous gases and the heat from the sun was too strong. The first plants lived in the nutrient-rich ocean more than 3 billion years ago.

About 400 mya, plants began to develop that were better able to inhabit the land. At first, plants grew close to the ground, but as more types developed, they had to compete for space and sunlight, so they adapted and grew taller. The primitive plants that developed thick, woody stems became the first trees.

When plants photosynthesize, they give off oxygen as a waste product. Because of this, early forests played a crucial role in the adaptations and survival of other organisms. The air was originally thick with gases, such as methane and ammonia, but no oxygen. Gradually, the forests put enough oxygen into the air for animals to develop and survive—a valuable service forests still provide today.

Over geologic time, plants evolved and adapted in order to survive. One example of successful adaptation is the tropical rain forests. The vegetation there has huge, wide leaves with the structure and ability to quickly eliminate excess water. Another example is a deciduous tree in a cool climate. Because trees cannot grow when the temperatures fall below freezing, they shed their leaves to protect against losing water. Some plants obtain their food and water from other plants by attaching huge sucking roots to them. These are called **parasites**. Some rain forest vines grow on existing trees; instead of having roots anchored into soil, they take water from the air around them and obtain minerals from decaying leaves in order to survive.

SEED DISPERSAL—THE STRATEGY TO LIVE

The success of a forest is directly linked to the ability of the vegetation—trees and other plants—to reproduce. Healthy reproduction enables the forest to be perpetuated over time. Nature has devised several ways for the seeds of plants to be dispersed. The success of a plant depends not only on the production of seed but also on the **dispersal** of that seed. Dispersal is the process by which plant species move into a new area. In order to survive, plants cannot just drop their seeds. If they did, the new seedlings would have to compete with the parent plant and with each other. Plants have developed a number of ways to increase the chances of their seeds being spread far enough away from the parent.

There are different types of seed dispersal mechanisms. The different mechanisms include wind, water, animals, and fire. The mechanism used depends on the habitat the plant is located in. The table on page 23 lists the different dispersal mechanisms and common seeds that are dispersed by that mechanism.

Wind Dispersal

Some seeds are carried to a new location by wind. Seeds travel the wind currents and gentle breezes with the potential of colonizing a distant mountain slope or valley. These seeds are very lightweight so that they can travel great distances. Many plants have developed ingenious adaptations for wind dispersal. They can resemble parachutes, helicopters, and gliders. There are several major types of wind dispersal that operate in forests:

- Gliders
- Parachutes
- Helicopters (whirlybirds)
- Flutterer/spinners
- Cottony seeds

Gliders include seeds with two wings that resemble the wings of an airplane. Parachutes have an umbrella-like crown of tiny hairs above a slender one-seeded fruit. These fragile seeds can become airborne

Seed Dispersal

Dispersal mechanism	Seed type
Wind	Dandelion, thistle, orchid, sycamore, poppy, ash, maple, grasses, milkweed, elm
Water	Coconut, water lily
Animals	Burdock (bur), blackberry, cherry, apple, acorn, tomato, watermelon, pumpkin, cedar
Fire	Lodgepole pine, jack pine, old man banksia

Seeds have developed many different dispersal mechanisms in order to maximize their chances of germination. Principal dispersal mechanisms include animal transport, wind, and mechanical transport. These seeds are from a maple tree and were transported by wind. *(Photo courtesy Nature's Images)*

with the slightest gust of wind. Milkweed and dandelion fluff are well-known examples of this type of wind dispersal.

Helicopters—also called whirlybirds—are seeds that have a single wing attached to the seed. Like a fan blade or propeller blade, the wing has a slight pitch to it, enabling the seed to spin as it falls. Depending on the wind velocity and distance above the ground, helicopter seeds can be carried long distances. Flutterer/spinners have papery wings that flutter and spin in the air and can be carried short distances by the wind.

Cottony seeds include seeds and tiny seed capsules with a tuft of cottony hairs at one end or seeds embedded in a cottony mass. Many plant families have this type of seed: the willow family, cottonwoods, cattail family, kapok tree, floss silk tree, and the sycamore family.

Water Dispersal

Fruits, such as the water lily and the coconut palm, are carried by water. Coconuts can travel for thousands of miles (km) across oceans. Biologists believe the original coconut palms on the South Sea islands (such as Tahiti, Samoa, Tonga, and Fiji) grew from fruits that were carried there from the main continents (such as South America) by ocean currents.

Animal Dispersal

Squirrels collect nuts, like acorns, and bury them for their winter food supply. If they forget about the seeds and do not eat them, the seeds have the potential to germinate and grow into oak trees. Other seeds can catch on the fur of animals and the feathers of birds and can be transported great distances—such as burs.

Fire

In order to survive wildfires, some plants have adaptive traits that allow them to reproduce (an adaptive trait is a characteristic that helps a plant survive and make the most of its habitat). Some plants have developed fire-adaptive traits that enable them to survive in areas prone to wild-fires. The intensity of the fire is crucial to the seed's dispersal—the fire must reach a certain temperature. The frequency of the fire is also important. Many species of pine trees have cones that only open after a fire. These pines are called serotinous.

The lodgepole pine—common in the western parts of the United States—is both serotinous and free-opening, which means that when the pine grows in an area where there are frequent fires, the cones are serotinous, but when it grows in an area where fires are less frequent, the cones open and release the seeds without the need for fire.

FOREST SUCCESSION

There are no stable communities of plants and animals. Many factors are constantly disrupting these ecosystems, such as food supply, climate, predation, and human encroachment. Conditions are favorable to different species at different times. Ecosystems are always in a state

Forest Succession

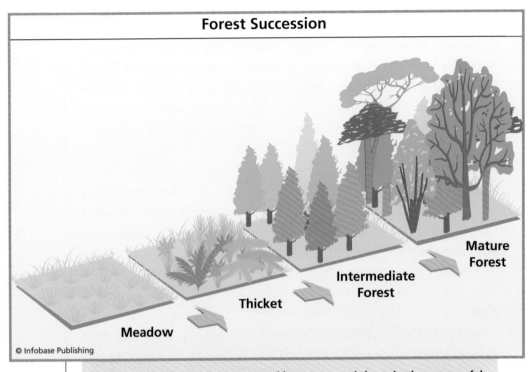

Mature
Forest

Intermediate
Forest

Thicket

Meadow

© Infobase Publishing

Forest succession: Areas start out with grasses, and then shrubs appear, followed by young forest and then mature forest.

of transition, always changing. Once an ecosystem has changed, it does not revert to previous conditions; it adapts accordingly.

The way in which cleared areas are recolonized by plants is called ecological **succession**. Different plants grow in different places, but the patterns of ecological succession are similar all over the world, in both temperate and tropical forests. First, the tough, **annual** grasses inhabit the area, followed by shrubs, and finally, after several years, trees. This is called a **climax** forest. A particular region has its own set of climax species, which are plants that are best adapted for the area and will persist after succession has finished, until another disturbance clears the area and the process starts over.

According to the U.S. Forest Service, the first species to move into an area are called **pioneer species** and need to be tough and grow quickly in order to survive in the often harsh conditions of recently distributed areas. The intermediate stages of vegetation are necessary for a new forest to grow. If an area is disturbed too often, the soil loses too many nutrients, and instead of returning to forest, the area remains a grassland.

In rain forests, the bushes and vines grow thickly and do not reach as high as the surrounding forest. In many areas, since the rain forest soil is so poor, repeated clearing of the forest will lead to severe soil depletion, and the normal patterns of succession will no longer occur. Instead of returning to a forest, the area will become a savanna (grassland) because there are not enough nutrients left in the soil to support trees.

There are many types of disturbances to forest ecosystems that cause change: some short term, some long term. A certain amount of disturbance is necessary to create habitat diversity. Examples of disturbances include small, frequent fires; changing weather conditions, such as cold temperatures or lack of water; or disease and infestation.

HUMAN IMPACTS ON FORESTS OVER THE CENTURIES

People have been cutting down forests for the past 10,000 years, and for many of the world's temperate forests, this marked the beginning of the end. Throughout time, human civilizations have had a significant impact on forest resources. As civilizations spread, huge areas of forest were consumed for timber, ships, buildings, and fuel for making bronze and iron as well as for heating dwellings. Everything from wheels and barrels to tool handles and furniture were made of wood. Because the temperate forest biome has rich, fertile soil, it has made some of the best farmland regions in the world. These areas have been converted to farmland for the past nine millennia.

Forests have also had an important role in history. For example, the island of Crete (in the Mediterranean) became a trading power and prosperous civilization mainly because of its forests. Wood was shipped to the Near East. The forests also provided fuel for working bronze and making pottery. Forests contributed to the development of Greece during the fifth century B.C. The wooden ships of Athens enabled the defeat of the Persians between 480 and 470 B.C.

Eventually, wood in Athens became scarce and expensive, which led Athens to obtain more through its conquest of other areas—a major reason for the Peloponnesian War. It was fought between Athens and Sparta and was largely a result of the desire to control timber supplies.

In the early 1600s, the English cut down the forests of Ireland to fuel their ironworks and build ships. The ironworks were using large amounts of wood harvested by the English to make cannons and sell them to foreign countries.

When the pilgrims arrived in America in 1620, the European settlers cut down many of the forests in order to farm. Within 200 years, very little forested area was left. Then, in the 1800s, new industries were invented and large cities began to develop. Many of the existing farms were abandoned, which were then, fortunately, able to revert back to forests.

The temperate forests today are the most densely populated biomes. Fortunately, people have begun to realize the value of forests, not only for the materials they provide, but for their beauty as well as the important role they play in the environment by providing oxygen and filtering water. In the United States, over a billion young trees are planted each year.

Rain forests have also been subjected to the effects of humans. Tropical rain forests once blanketed the Earth in a wide distribution around the equator. A few thousand years ago, scientists believe rain forests covered 14% of the Earth's land surface—roughly 7.8 million square miles (20.2 million sq. km). Humans have destroyed half of the rain forest area, with the most significant damage occurring in the last two centuries. Today only 2.5 million square miles (6.5 million sq. km) of tropical rain forest remain. Scientists estimate that about 93,000 square miles (240,870 sq. km) are lost every year.

It is not only the quantity of life that is threatened but also the diversity of life that has been impacted that makes deforestation so

The tropical rain forest is home to a diverse number of plant and animal species, such as this torch ginger. *(Photo courtesy Nature's Images)*

tragic. Rain forests play a vital role in the Earth's environment. Some of the most unique and most beautiful plants and animals are found in the rain forest.

Rain forests are being affected by timber removal, mining for minerals, agriculture, ranching, and human settlement. Most attempts to turn tropical rain forest into farmland have failed, resulting in damaged soil and disrupted water systems. The bulk of the nutrients are in the biomass (living matter, such as plants) rather than in the soil. To remove the biomass also removes the nutrients. Tragically, areas that are clearcut to farm can only be used a short while before they are rendered infertile and useless.

When rain forests are **threatened**, much more than just land is lost. Intact tropical rain forests have many intangible benefits that are also impacted, such as wildlife habitat, their job as a major role in the Earth's water cycle, and a storage area for carbon which helps combat the current issues of global warming.

The Disappearing Rain Forests

- Rain forests once covered 14% of the Earth's land surface; now they cover only 6%, and experts estimate that the last remaining rain forests could be consumed in less than 40 years.
- Most rain forests are cleared by chain saws, bulldozers, and fires for their timber value and are then used for farming and ranching operations.
- There were an estimated 10 million Indians living in the Amazonian rain forest 500 years ago. Today, there are fewer than 200,000.
- Nearly half of the world's species of plants, animals, and microorganisms will be destroyed or severely threatened over the next quarter century due to rain forest deforestation.
- Experts estimate that we are losing 137 plant, animal, and insect species every single day due to rain forest deforestation. That equates to 50,000 species a year. As the rain forest species disappear, so do many possible cures for life-threatening diseases. Approximately 25% of Western pharmaceuticals are derived from rain forest ingredients, but less than 1% of the tropical trees and plants in the rain forest have been tested so far by scientists. These plants need to be studied before they become extinct.

(Source: Raintree Nutrition, Inc.)

THE IMPORTANCE OF BIODIVERSITY

Biological diversity refers to all of the different kinds of life on Earth. Also called biodiversity, biological diversity is often used to refer to the total number of different species on Earth. Estimates of the number of species on Earth range from 5 to 7 million, but some scientists estimate there are as many as 30 million.

Much of the Earth's biodiversity is concentrated in the tropics. Some scientists estimate that 50% of all species on the planet are found in tropical rain forests that comprise only 7% of the Earth's land surface. With the rapid rate at which tropical rain forests are being cut, it is estimated that up to 20% of the Earth's biodiversity may become extinct in the next few decades.

According to the David Suzuki Foundation, some scientists believe that the accumulation of **greenhouse gases** in the atmosphere may lead to the alteration of long-term weather patterns. The resulting changes in climate might be one of the biggest threats to biodiversity.

Healthy ecosystems have high biodiversity. Having a wide diversity of life on Earth is valuable for many reasons, such as ecological values, economic values, and cultural values. All living creatures are supported by the interactions among organisms and ecosystems. Loss of biodiversity makes ecosystems less stable and more vulnerable to extreme events and weakens its natural cycles.

Loss of biodiversity means humans would not only lose enriched, intriguing ecosystems, but also lose plants and other organisms that could improve or benefit everyone's lives. For example, the tropical forests have provided humankind with food crops on a daily basis, such as peppers, corn, tomatoes, rice, coconuts, bananas, coffee, cocoa, beans, and sweet potatoes. Tropical biodiversity has also provided humans with many medicines used to treat such diseases as malaria and cancer. According to the Missouri Botanical Garden, without maintaining the natural diversity of an area, things may be lost before they have even been discovered. The importance, and role, of biodiversity will be emphasized more throughout the chapters of this book.

RENEWABLE AND NONRENEWABLE RESOURCES

There are two general classes of resources: renewable and nonrenewable. This chapter will focus on the various forest resources, the importance of biodiversity and renewability, soil resources, water resources, human and cultural resources, unique plant and animal life in the forest, and forest ecology and the treasure of old-growth forests.

TYPES OF FOREST RESOURCES AND THE IMPORTANCE OF RENEWABILITY

A renewable resource is a resource that can be replenished. It is a resource that can be replaced through natural ecological cycles and/or good management practices. The opposite of this is a nonrenewable resource—a resource that cannot be replenished (once it is gone, it is gone forever). For practical applications, some scientists consider a renewable resource one that can be replenished within one generation of a human's lifetime (about 20 to 30 years).

For many classes of resources, it is easy to determine which resources are renewable and which are not. For example, with energy resources, fossil fuels (oil and petroleum) and coal are not renewable because they took millions of years to form. Even though the same geologic processes are still happening today, these resources will never be replaced within a human lifetime. Energy resources, such as wind and water power, are considered renewable because they are readily abundant and can be generated within a short time period.

Forest resources involve ecosystems, which are fragile and complex. All elements of living systems are interwoven; if one element is affected, the entire system is affected. Compare these interactions to a car: A car will work well as long as all the individual components are being taken care of and functioning right; but if one of the parts is neglected or damaged and stops working properly—for example, if the engine runs out of oil—it impacts the entire system. If one component stops working the way it should, the entire system is jeopardized, and until that one component is managed correctly and repaired, the system fails or is unproductive.

Forests are a highly valuable resource. They are the basis of a healthy ecosystem and perform important functions, such as purifying the air and water. Humans, and other life, depend on the oxygen that is given off as a by-product from photosynthesis in plants. Forests are also important in the water cycle—more than 90% of the water that is taken in through a plant's roots is eventually released back to the atmosphere in a process called **transpiration**.

Forests provide protection and shelter by providing wood to construct homes. They also provide shelter and habitat for many other animals as well. For example, a single tree in the rain forest can be a home to more than 1,000 different insect species. Forests are also the source of many medicinal products people use every day, such as aspirin.

Although it may seem that forests are renewable, that may not be the case. For example, if an aggressive plant or weed infests an area, it can crowd out the native (natural) plants by choking them out or using vital nutrients in the soil that native plants need to survive. Whatever the reason, if native plants are removed and the invasive plants take over, the native plants have become nonrenewable in that area as long as those conditions persist.

THE VALUE AND IMPORTANCE OF BIODIVERSITY

Healthy forests—tropical, temperate, and boreal—are not composed of just one ecosystem, but some, such as rain forests, host millions of unique ecosystems—from that found in a single tree to those in an entire forest. They represent rich reservoirs and key components of the diversity of life on Earth. For example, tropical rain forests are home to over half the world's species, all confined within a narrow strip of land around the equator. The abundant sunlight, warm temperatures, and daily rain lead to a fast turnover of nutrients, and because of this, plant growth is rapid. Because they do not have winters, the growing season lasts all year. There are flowers and fruit all year round. The rain forests provide a home for millions of humans that have been a part of forest ecosystems for thousands of years. They also provide a home for some of the most unique animal and plant species on Earth.

As mentioned in the previous chapter, having a wide diversity of life on Earth is valuable for many reasons—some more obvious than others. Loss of biodiversity makes ecosystems less stable, more vulnerable to extreme events, and weakens natural cycles.

The energy cycle that exists in forests is one important value humans benefit from. Photosynthesis—the process by which green plants convert sunlight, water, nutrients, and **carbon dioxide** into carbohydrates—releases oxygen into the atmosphere. Plants and photosynthetic bacteria transform energy from the sun into stored chemical energy, which is the foundation for virtually all food webs on Earth.

Forests also provide a major role in the water cycle. This refers to the circulation, transformation, and replenishment of freshwater from all of Earth's ecosystems. Forests moderate water flow by catching, holding, and recycling rainwater. Plants release absorbed rainwater into the air through the loss of water through their leaves, which is called transpiration. Forests also play a major part in the water and other cycles, which is discussed in more detail in Chapter 4.

Although people may think these important services that forests provide are renewable, that may not be the case. If the environment becomes polluted or damaged by overuse, it can negatively impact these valuable resources.

There are also economic values of forests that may or may not be renewable. Today, the world's food supply is derived from about 30 crops and 14 animal species. Because humans depend on so few plant and animal species for survival, they are vulnerable to environmental changes or crop diseases.

Scientists have identified about 270,000 species of plants; but many scientists believe the total number of plant species could be as high as 320,000 worldwide. New species are discovered each year in the rain forest, and scientists believe that not even half of the existing species have been described yet. Many of these organisms have remained unknown because of the remoteness of their habitat. For instance, many rain forest species live only at the tops of tall trees, unseen from the ground; while others live about halfway to the top, making it difficult to study them. Other areas are hard to study because of their remote geographical locations. In the rain forests alone, because of their biodiversity, scientists think there may be over 1,600 tropical forest plants that have the potential to be grown as vegetable crops.

Rain forest plants are also a source of present and potential medicines. Plants are the source of medications such as aspirin, heart stimulants, antibiotics, and antimalarial and cancer-fighting compounds. For example, a drug called **Taxol**—derived from the Pacific yew tree—has shown promise in the treatment of ovarian and breast cancers.

More than 120 prescription drugs are derived from higher plants; yet less than 1% of rain forest plants have been tested for their medicinal properties. It has been estimated that of the world's 270,000 known plant species, only 5,000 have been tested for their medicinal potential. In the United States, more than $6 billion a year is spent on medicines derived from tropical plants. If forest resources are

Rain Forest Facts

- The Amazon rain forest covers over a billion acres in Venezuela, Brazil, Ecuador, Peru, and Colombia.
- More than half of the world's estimated 10 million species of plants, animals, and insects live in the tropical rain forests. One-fifth of the world's freshwater is in the Amazon basin.
- At least 80% of the developed world's diet originates in the tropical rain forest. It provides foods such as figs, lemons, oranges, guavas, bananas, grapefruit, avocados, coconuts, pineapples, mangos, tomatoes, corn, potatoes, rice, yams, black pepper, cayenne, chocolate, cloves, cinnamon, sugarcane, ginger, turmeric, vanilla, Brazil nuts, coffee, and cashews.
- At least 3,000 fruits are found in the rain forests. Today, the Western world uses about 200. The native inhabitants of the rain forest use more than 2,000.
- Currently, 121 prescription drugs sold worldwide come from plant-derived sources. Approximately 25% of Western pharmaceuticals are derived from rain forest ingredients, but less than 1% of these tropical trees and plants have been tested by scientists for their therapeutic benefits.
- The U.S. Cancer Institute has identified 3,000 plants that are active against cancer cells. Of these, 70% are found in the rain forest. Twenty-five percent of the active ingredients in today's cancer-fighting drugs come from organisms found only in the rain forest.
- In 1983, there were no U.S. pharmaceutical manufacturers involved in research programs to discover new drugs or cures from plants. Today, more than 100 pharmaceutical companies and several branches of the U.S. government, including major companies like Merck and the National Cancer Institute, are involved in plant research projects for possible drugs and cures for infections, cancer, and AIDS.

(Sources: Raintree Nutrition, Inc. and the Rainforest Alliance).

not protected, much in the way of useful resources now and in the future will be lost—making them nonrenewable. It is hard to put a value on these renewable resources that are essential for the quality of life that exists today. These resources play a role in climate regulation; water purification; soil regeneration; nutrient cycling; waste recirculation; and production of timber, fodder, and biomass. These services are provided by the living environment for free—these resources just need to be managed properly and conserved in order to remain renewable.

SOIL RESOURCES

Fertile soil is one of the lands' most important natural resources, because everything that lives on land depends directly or indirectly on soil. For example, without soil, farmers could not grow plants, which means they could not grow food for animals or people.

Soil is considered a nonrenewable resource because it is created so slowly that it can take hundreds of years for just a few inches (cm) to form. A well-developed soil that is extremely fertile could have taken thousands of years to develop. Because of this, soil resources must be well-managed. If nutrients are removed, or the soil is eroded or overused, vegetation will not grow well.

Soil is much more than just dirt. The type of soil and what actually goes on in the soil determine how well plants grow. Five factors determine what types of soil form on Earth: (1) parent material (what the soil is made from), (2) organisms (that live in the soil), (3) topography (how steep or level the land is), (4) climate (which heats, cools, wets, and dries soil), and (5) time (the longer the time, the more developed the soil becomes).

Soil protects plant roots from exposure to the sun's heat. It also filters pollution that comes from rain and water runoff. Plants utilize soil to grow and receive support while they grow.

Soil also has other important components. It must contain water, air pockets, and microorganisms. Tiny organisms live on decaying plants in the soil, turning the plants into **humus**. Humus makes soil more productive because it absorbs heat, holds more moisture, and provides food for the plants.

Soil produces almost all our food and fiber. Soil provides 13 of the 16 essential nutrients needed for plant growth. It provides nitrogen, phosphorus, calcium, sulfur, copper, boron, zinc, manganese, molybdenum, chlorine, iron, magnesium, and potassium. These nutrients come from the weathered minerals and decayed plant matter found in the soil. Carbon, hydrogen, and oxygen are stored in the air spaces between soil particles.

Soil also helps filter and purify water. When water travels over or through soil before entering rivers or lakes, the soil helps prevent flooding by allowing excess water to soak in for use by plants or to percolate (flow through) to other underground water bodies (called aquifers). Soil helps purify contaminated water by removing the impurities and killing potential disease-causing organisms. Soil is important because it recycles dead plants and animals into the nutrients needed by all living things. It also exchanges gases, which keep resource cycles going.

If forests and their soils are well-managed, the health of the forests is protected. This especially applies to the temperate deciduous and coniferous forests. The difference between the soils of the rain forests and temperate forests is striking. The rain forest exists through nutrient recycling. In a rain forest, the soil is extremely poor and cannot always supply the nutrients required for plant growth. As plants die, their parts are quickly decomposed, and the next generation of plants recycles the nutrients they contained. Competition for the minerals is fierce. If a leaf falls from a tall tree, or a piece of fruit is knocked off a branch and falls to the forest floor, the detritivores (bacteria and fungi that break down dead material) immediately get to work and start digesting the fallen piece of organic matter.

The detritivores' digestive processes make the minerals available again, and the net of shallow plant roots soaks them up and sends them up into the trees and vines. This nutrient recycling is very efficient because all the elements are reused as soon as they become available.

Nothing is wasted. If the rain forest is cut down, nothing remains but a thin layer of low fertility soil.

A major problem in the rain forest is the rapid removal of the trees, clearing the land for agriculture, or grazing. Because the soil is so thin, it is difficult to grow crops. In addition, many of the rain forest soils are acidic, which stunts root development in plants. There are also a lot of clays, which contain aluminum that is toxic to plants. Because of this, the soils become depleted of nutrients in a very short time period, leaving the land infertile.

The result of widespread cutting is to completely remove the nutrients from the area, often making recovery impossible. It also allows erosion of the clays to occur, choking the waters with silt. For these reasons, soil is a resource that must be carefully managed in order to maintain its health.

WATER RESOURCES

Forests play a critical role for water resources. The sheer density of trees in the rain forest directly affects global moisture and heat distribution. The excessive amounts of rainfall they receive plays a major role in the Earth's water budget. In fact, rain forests are so humid, that the forests at higher elevations are always covered in clouds—called cloud forests.

Rain forests are subject to heavy rainfall, receiving between 79 inches (200 cm) and 430 inches (1,902 cm) of rain each year. In equatorial regions, rainfall can be year-round; other rain forests have a "wet" and "dry" season. "Dry" is a relative term, however. In seasonal forests the period between rains is usually not long enough for the ground to completely dry out. During the "drier" parts of the year, the constant cloud cover is enough to keep the air moist and prevent plants from drying out.

The moisture of the rain forest from the combined effects of rain, cloud cover, and transpiration (water loss through leaves) creates an extreme local humidity. In fact, each canopy tree transpires about 200 gallons (760 liters) of water annually, equaling about 20,000 gallons

The rain forests play an important role in providing for the world's water resources. Thick vegetation and waterfalls are found throughout the rain forests. *(Photo courtesy Nature's Images)*

(76,000 L) of water transpired into the atmosphere for every acre of canopy trees. The humidity can become so great that it forms rain clouds and provides three-fourths of the rain it receives—a form of a self-generating, recyclable water supply. Scientists have determined that the rain forests in the Amazon create nearly half of their own precipitation. One thing that has experts worried is the notion that deforestation and climate change may adversely affect the water cycle in tropical rain forests.

Forests in temperate areas—such as in the United States—also play important roles, including protecting streams and rivers. Forests that

Some areas of the rain forest are cloud forests—areas where mountain peaks are almost constantly draped in clouds. *(Photo courtesy Nature's Images)*

border streams are called riparian buffers, or streamside forests. They are crucial to the protection and enhancement of water resources. They are complex ecosystems that provide food and habitat for stream communities, as well as help in controlling pollution and erosion.

Streamside forests provide many benefits to the quality of water resources. They remove excess nutrients and sediment from surface water runoff and shallow groundwater. They also help shade streams to optimize light and temperature conditions for aquatic plants and animals. Streamside forests filter pesticides and keep them out of the water.

Streamside forests function as filters, transformers, sinks, and sources. For example, they provide better conditions for plants and animals, thereby increasing biological diversity. They filter by removing sediment and other suspended solids from surface runoff. For example, according to U.S. National Fish and Wildlife Service, cropland erosion accounts for 38% of the 1.5 billion tons of sediment that reach America's rivers each year. Pasture and range erosion account for another 26%.

It is important that these sediments get filtered out because sediment in the water can block out sunlight, harming the plant growth in the area. Sediment deposited on the bottom of the streambed can interfere with the feeding and reproduction of bottom-dwelling fish and aquatic insects, weakening the food chain. Huge amounts of sediments dumped into streams can cause floods because they cause the stream to leave its banks. The forest helps stop sediments from flowing into streams and rivers by blocking them with trees and forest litter and filtering sediments through the soil.

Excess nitrogen from animal waste, particularly in agricultural areas, can reach streams with runoff. Bacteria and fungi in the streamside forest dissolve excess nitrogen into various nitrogen gases, returning it to the atmosphere. According to the Natural Resources Conservation Service (NRCS), studies have shown that the amount of nitrogen in runoff and shallow groundwater can be reduced by as much as 80% after passing through a streamside forest. The same is true for many toxic chemicals, such as pesticides, because bacteria and fungi help convert toxic chemicals to nontoxic forms.

Streamside forests act as a sink by storing nutrients for extended periods of time because the nutrients are taken up by plants and stored in plant tissue. Some scientists say that 25% of the nitrogen removed by

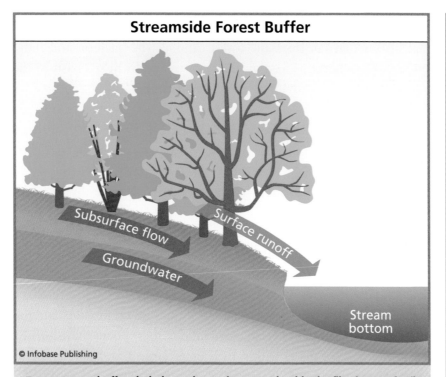

Streamside Forest Buffer

Subsurface flow

Surface runoff

Groundwater

Stream bottom

© Infobase Publishing

Forest stream buffers help keep the environment healthy by filtering out fertilizers, pesticides, and sediment. They also store nutrients that contribute to the overall health of plants in the area.

the streamside forest is taken into tree growth, which is stored for long periods of time in the wood. Nitrogen and other nutrients can also be passed up the food chain when plants are eaten by animals. In wetter areas, nutrients in leaf litter can be stored for longer periods as peat. Nutrients can be filtered, transformed, or stored by processes taking place in the forest litter.

Streamside forests also provide a source of energy for aquatic life because they provide dissolved carbon compounds and an organic particle mixture called detritus. These minerals help restore and maintain nature's equilibrium in small, well-shaded upland streams. According to the NRCS, as much as 75% of the organic food base may be supplied by dissolved organic compounds or detritus such as fruit, limbs, leaves, and insects that fall from the forest canopy. The bacteria and fungi on the stream bottoms feed on the detritus and form the basis of the aquatic food chain, providing for a diversity of life.

HUMAN AND CULTURAL RESOURCES

An important resource tied directly to forests—especially rain forests—is the people who live there. They are often called the forest people. Today, there are about a thousand different tribes living in the rain forests around the world.

Many indigenous people have shaped civilizations and cultures based on the environments in which they live. Great civilizations like the Mayas, Incas, and Aztecs developed complex societies and made great contributions to science. Living from nature and lacking technology, native people learned to watch their surroundings and understand the intricacies of the rain forest. Over generations, these people have learned the importance of living within their environment and have come to rely on the multitude of renewable benefits that forests can provide.

Lifestyles for indigenous people vary. Although some live similarly to the developed world, others still live much as their ancestors did thousands of years ago. Many rely on the rain forest for food, medicine, and clothing. Because they know that misuse of the resources will threaten their survival, tribal members practice rainforest sustainability (not taking more than they need). These people are community-oriented—taught skills by their families and others in the community. Many tribes have experienced death and disease upon contact with the outside world. Their immune systems have no resistance to diseases they have never been exposed to, and when they come in contact with new people they are extremely vulnerable.

In addition to fishing, hunting, and gathering wild fruits and nuts, indigenous people also plant small gardens, using a sustainable farming method called **shifting cultivation**. They begin by clearing a small area of land and burning it. Then they plant many types of plants to be used as food or medicine. After a few years, the ground becomes infertile, so they abandon that site and move to another area and start again. Shifting cultivation is still practiced by those who have access to large amounts of land.

Some of the best known tribes today are the Baka, Yanomamo, Efe Pygmy, Kayapo, Cashinahau, Maroons, and Tukano. The Baka, a tribe in Africa, live in green-domed structures made out of Tilipi leaves. During the rainy season, they travel in search of food. In the dry season, they return to live in their villages. The Yanamamo reside deep in the Amazon. They live solitary, isolated lives. They were unknown until the 1950s, when they were finally discovered. They are very adept at hunting and growing fruit. One of the main staples of this tribe is the plantain, a banana-type fruit.

The Efe Pygmies are some of the smallest people in the world, usually not growing any taller than four feet eight inches (142 cm). They exist in rain forests throughout the African continent. The Kayapo tribe lives in the Amazon River Basin of Brazil. They have a very symbolic culture and adorn themselves with colorful body paints. The Cashinahau tribe lives in Peru. In keeping with their customs, many have body piercings and wear body paint. Their homes are crude structures made of natural materials, such as leaves and sticks held together by mud.

The Maroons are found in the rain forests of Africa. Scientists believe this tribe represents the descendants of slaves that escaped generations earlier. They live a very quiet family-oriented lifestyle along the river. Often a family will pass its plantations down from generation to generation. The Tukano lives in Northwest Brazil. The Tukano is one large tribe, made up of several smaller groups. They principally reside in small houses made from palm leaves. Their society is closely structured. Their settlements have a large communal building in the center, with houses around it and farming areas beyond the houses. They have a communal lifestyle—all inhabitants pitch in and help with work that needs to be done. Unfortunately, as big businesses have been allowed to come into the rain forest to cut trees, ranch, and mine, many native dwellers have lost their homes.

A Kayapo medicine man (shaman) in the Amazon rain forest in Brazil. *(Image from Mongabay.com, photo by Sue Wren)*

The knowledge that these tribes possess is an extremely valuable resource. Besides having unique cultures that everyone can learn from, they also possess an enormous body of almost irreplaceable information about the rain forest and how to live there without destroying it. If these cultures disappear, then their unique knowledge of the rain forest will disappear also.

UNIQUE PLANT AND ANIMAL LIFE IN THE FOREST

Plant and animal life in the forest is diverse, with each species adapted to its environment and filling a specific niche in the ecosystem. The world's rain forests are full of an extraordinary variety of plant life.

Vegetation in the rain forests grows to huge proportions. These Amazon lilies can grow to as much as 6 feet (1.8 m) in diameter. *(Courtesy of U.S. National Oceanic and Atmospheric Administration, photo by Commander John Bortniak)*

Scientists estimate there are more than 80,000 flowering plants in the Amazon alone, which in turn support an estimated 30 million animal species, mainly insects. The rain forests located in Africa, South America, and Southeast Asia contain about 180,000 species of plants. The majority—about 67%—of all plant species that exist on Earth occur in the rain forests.

Many of the plants that are related to other species in other parts of the world are huge in size compared to their cousins because the rain forest behaves like an immense hothouse. For example, the giant Amazon water lily has leaves that grow to more than 6 feet (2 m) in diameter—large enough that a small child can float in it like a raft.

Rain forests contain a wide variety of unique plants found nowhere else in the world. Even though each plant species occupies a specific niche in the ecosystem, there is competition to survive and reproduce. This has forced many thousands of plants to evolve in ways that take advantage of certain rain forest conditions.

Because of this competition, many scientists believe that the reason there are so many plant species is that they have had to adapt in order to survive. Many plants have adapted in unique ways. For instance, some plants contain substances that are poisonous to insects and other predators in order to keep from being eaten. But the insects and other predators evolve and adapt by slowly becoming resistant to the poisons. In order for the plant to survive—and not go extinct—they must further adapt to ward off the evolved insects.

Other plants can be pollinated by only one species of insect. For example, in Madagascar, the white orchid produces a large flower with an unusually long, thin tube. The nectar is contained at the end of the tube. The length of the tube prevents most insects from pollinating it, except for a single species of moth, whose tongue happens to extend 18 inches (45 cm). Only this insect can pollinate the white orchid.

Each rain forest around the world contains many hundreds of plant species that are unique to just that rain forest—these are called endemic plants. In fact, a single acre of rain forest can contain more than 300 different species of trees.

Some of the characteristic rain forest plant life includes bromeliads, which are related to the pineapple family. Their leaves are thick and waxy; at the base of the plant, the leaves form a hollow bowl. This is an example of an adaptation of the species that allows them to hold large amounts of water—up to several gallons at a time.

Epiphytes are another interesting species. These plants are able to grow anywhere—such as on branches, trunks, or another tree's foliage. They do not need soil in which to grow. Because they can be found growing from branches high up in the rainforest canopy, they are often referred to as "air plants." There are many different types of epiphytes, all of which may grow on the same tree. Examples include

Many plant species are found only in the world's rain forests, some only in a very narrow geographic area. This bromeliad species grows in Kauai, Hawaii. *(Photo courtesy Nature's Images)*

orchids, cactuses, bromeliads, aroids, lichens, mosses, and ferns. In order to begin growth high up in the forest canopy, their seeds must be transported to that location—usually by wind or birds.

Buttress roots are another interesting species in the rain forest. Unlike other fertile farming areas around the world, where the soil is deep and rich in nutrients, rain forest soils are very thin and contain very few nutrients. Because of this, the tree's roots do not extend down very far into the soil profile, but instead, spread outward just under the surface of the ground. Because these trees are so tall, they need extra support to keep them from falling over. Buttress roots perform this

The soil is so shallow, and the trees so tall in the rain forest, that many require support from buttress roots, which act like stilts to stabilize and support the trees. *(Photo by Rhett Butler, Mongabay.com)*

function. They are large roots that grow like stilts from the bottom of the trees. Often very thick, they prop the tree up and give it stability. They come in many different sizes—some as high as 15 feet (4.6 m) above the ground.

Lianas are a type of climbing vine found throughout the tropical rain forests. They have thick, woody stems and come in various lengths (up to 3,000 feet, or 914 m) and varying shapes. They start growing on the forest floor, but because the forest floor is usually dark (sunlight cannot penetrate the thick foliage in the canopies above), they begin to climb the trees, like snakes, in search of sunlight. These are the jungle vines made popular in Tarzan movies. They do this by attaching themselves to trees with sucker roots, or tendrils, and growing with the young sapling, or they climb by winding themselves around the tree's trunk. Liana species include rattan palms, philodendrons, and *Strychnos toxifera* (from which the deadly poison strychnine is obtained). Rattans are used to make things like baskets, ropes, and wicker furniture.

Saprophytes play an extremely important role. They are the organisms that act as the rain forest's decomposers. These fungi, which resemble mushroom-type growths, are very efficient at accelerating **decomposition**. For example, they can break down dead animals and vegetation within 24 hours. Through their process of decomposition they add important nutrients to the soil, such as potassium, phosphorus, calcium, and iron—all important elements necessary for the growth of healthy plants.

There are also carnivorous (meat-eating) plants in the rain forest. These plants acquire their nutrients from animal matter. Two of the most well-known varieties of carnivorous plants are the Venus fly trap and the pitcher plant. The pitcher plant can grow to be 30 feet (9 m) tall and can have pitcher-shaped flowers—usually 12 inches (30 cm) long—which are usually stuffed full of the bodies of the insects they have eaten. Besides insects, they have been known to even eat small mammals and reptiles that were unlucky enough to fall into the pitcher.

Orchids are one of the most abundant and varied of the flowering plant families in the rain forest. In fact, there are over 20,000 species. Some orchids grow in the soil, others function as epiphytes that grow on other trees. Many of the diverse species of flowering plants in the rain forest are very beautiful.

The plants in the temperate forests include both deciduous and coniferous trees, such as maple, oak, hickory, aspen, pine, ponderosa, piñon, juniper, and redwood. Some of the most-often visited temperate forests in the world are found along the Pacific Coast from central California to southern Oregon. The beautiful, awe-inspiring redwood forests in northern California are coniferous forests that millions of people visit each year as a vacation destination. Some of the giant sequoias reach heights of 350 feet (107 m)—the height of a 35-story building—and can weigh more than 6,000 tons (5,443 metric tons).

Many of the flowers in the rain forest are unique to specific areas. A wide array of unusual and beautiful flowers are abundant. More are just waiting to be discovered. *(Photo courtesy Nature's Images)*

America's redwoods and sequoias are famous worldwide for their size and age.

Similar to the rain forests, temperate and boreal forests also have layers of vegetation. They are not as biodiverse, however (they provide habitat for fewer species than the rain forests). The first level, the forest floor, consists of dead leaves, moss, lichen, and rotting wood. A multitude of insects, spiders, worms, and soil bacteria also live there.

The shrub and herb layer makes up the second level of the forest. Growing in this layer are woody shrubs, berry bushes, ferns, wildflowers, and grasses. Birds, insects, and ground-dwelling animals—such as mice, foxes, bears, snakes, chipmunks, pikas, and squirrels—are found in this layer. The top two layers are the canopy and the understory. The canopy contains the oldest and tallest trees, and the understory contains shorter

Many tropical flowers are popular not only in the wild, but in decorative gardens and flower arrangements, as is this hibiscus. *(Photo courtesy Nature's Images)*

The rafflesia is the largest flower in the world, found in rain forest areas like Malaysia. The bloom has been known to reach a diameter of 3 feet (1 m). These flowers are becoming threatened because of overharvesting. *(Courtesy Lost World Arts, photo by Karl Lehmann)*

trees and saplings. Often the trees in the understory must compete for sunlight if the tallest trees are dense.

All levels are important to the health of the forests. It is a working system, each part important in its own way. If components of the forest are removed—such as from deforestation, disease, drought, invasive species, **acid rain**, pollution, and other destructive factors—those components can become nonrenewable resources. This can have a domino effect on the rest of the forest, because all components are related to, and depend on, other components. If vegetation becomes nonrenewable, the forest may become a nonrenewable resource. One example of this is deforestation of the rain forest. Once it is deforested, it is unlikely that rain forest will be renewed, because the soil does not contain enough nutrients to allow for that.

Forests also support diverse populations of animals. This is especially true in the rain forest. For example, a 4-square-mile (10-sq.-km) area contains about 125 mammal species, 400 bird species, 60 **amphibian**

The Original Chocolate Factory

The cacao tree is an evergreen that grows to about 15 to 25 feet (5 to 8 m). The fruits and flowers of the cacao tree grow directly from its trunk. The tree grows an oblong fruit—called a pod—that can be 4 to 12 inches (10 to 30 cm) long. The green pods turn yellow, red, or purple when they are ripe. Each pod contains 20 to 60 reddish brown cocoa beans that are as much as an inch (2.5 cm) long. The pods are harvested at the end of the rainy season. It takes about 7 to 14 pods to produce 1 pound (0.45 kilogram) of dry cocoa beans.

Cocoa originated in the lowland rain forests of the Amazon River basins of South America. Today, it is found as far north as southern Mexico. The end product of cocoa beans is chocolate.

Humans have eaten chocolate since as far back as 600 B.C., when the first hot chocolate drink was made from mashed cocoa seeds. Today, cocoa is a major cultivated food crop from the rain forests.

Animals on the forest floor of the rain forests adapt to hide in their environment, as does this jaguar in a reserve area in Belize. *(Photo by Rhett Butler, Mongabay.com)*

Parrots are plentiful in the rain forests, such as this rainbow lorikeet, which lives in the rain forests of Australia. *(Photo by Rhett Butler, Mongabay.com)*

This is a red pitcher plant (*Nepenthes rafflesiana*) in the rain forest of Kalimantan (Indonesian Borneo). The pitcher plant is carnivorous. It has a sticky liquid at the bottom. When insects come in to the flower for the nectar, the insect slips down the slick inside "pitcher-shaped" portion of the flower and cannot climb back up. Once the insect is trapped, the plant ingests it. *(Photo by Rhett Butler, Mongabay.com)*

species, 100 reptile species, and over 150 butterfly species. There are also tens of thousands of insect species.

Life in the rain forests is so diverse because different species live in different levels of the forest, oftentimes undetected because of special adaptations such as camouflage. Some species protect themselves by being poisonous, such as spiders, snakes, and frogs.

Rain forests provide homes to many large bird species, such as the macaw. Oftentimes, it is hard to see all the birds in the forest. This is because the rain forest trees are so tall, with more of their branches and leaves far above the forest floor, which is where most of the birds are—in the dense **foliage**, out of sight. Rain forest animals include boa constrictors, anacondas, pythons, macaws, hornbills, toucans, orangutans, gorillas, chimpanzees, bats, sloths, lemurs, and leopards.

Temperate and boreal forests also host distinctive wildlife. Animals in these forests must adapt to cool temperatures and dry conditions because these forests have greater temperature extremes. Different birds, animals, and insects make use of the various forest layers for food, water,

Parrots and Macaws

Parrots and macaws are highly social birds found in almost every tropical forest in the world. There are 337 species in the parrot order and family, which includes macaws, cockatoos, lories, and lorikeets. The tiniest are the 3-inch (8 cm) pigmy parrots, and the largest—the macaws—are about 40 inches (102 cm) in length. Mid-sized species of the New World are usually referred to as parrots. Green is the predominant parrot color, making them difficult to see in the treetops, but many species also have bright rainbow hues.

Parrots' bills are adapted for prying open hard nuts, chomping on fruits, and grinding seeds. Their legs are short and strong, and with their bills, they are excellent climbers. Due mainly to deforestation and the illegal pet trade, one-fourth of the parrot species are in danger of extinction.

Mule deer are common in the temperate forests of the United States. *(Photo by Gary Kramer, courtesy of Natural Resources Conservation Service)*

and shelter. Because the upper layers of forests receive the most sunlight, they produce more food, which is why many of the birds, insects, and animals that eat fruit, nuts, and leaves spend most of their time in the canopy and understory layers. Animals that live in these forests include eagles, hawks, cougars (mountain lions), bobcats, deer, elk, moose, caribou, bears, wolves, beavers, mice, porcupines, skunks, and owls.

Just as plants can become nonrenewable, so can the animal species that inhabit the forests. If they are hunted, captured, become exposed to disease, **endangered** by invasive species or humans, or have the vegetation that they depend on as a food source removed, they can quickly become nonrenewable resources.

FOREST ECOLOGY

As this chapter has illustrated, forests are much more than trees. Part of what makes forests amazing is the complex relationships between flora and fauna. The trees, plants, mosses, lichens, insects, and animals are all essential forest elements. If any of these components disappear, the overall health of the forest is jeopardized.

An outstanding example of a working forest ecology can be seen in old-growth forests. A forest becomes old growth when it develops for hundreds of years without any major disturbance, such as a forest fire or logging. Many of the majestic forests in the Pacific Northwest are old-growth forests. When a forest grows a long time with only small disturbances, it develops into a very different ecosystem from a young forest. Some of them in the United States have been growing since the Revolutionary War in the 1700s. Others are over 1,000 years old.

Old-growth forests also have multiple layers. Shrubs and young trees grow on old decaying logs, as well as the ground. Even the trees have other plants growing on them, such as mosses and ferns.

The complexity of the old-growth forest—its many diverse layers—is an important part of what makes an old-growth forest unique. Scientists have found that these forests support many more species of plants and animals than younger forests do. Some species are only found in old-growth forests (an endemic species).

An old-growth forest usually has a different climate at the treetops than it does on the forest floor. They also have a lot of **snags**—dead trees that are still standing. Snags provide essential habitat for many animal species. Some function as their own local ecosystem. They also serve as a storehouse for nutrients.

One reason that old-growth trees get so big is because they live a long time. These trees can be 500 to 1,000 years old. These trees are also resilient and can often survive a forest fire. Their bark may become blackened in a fire, but the bark is so thick, it protects the tree's inner wood from damage. The wood also stores organic materials and nutrients. Even after the tree dies, its wood will be used for hundreds of years by many plants and animals, serving as a renewable resource.

CHAPTER 4

DEVELOPMENT OF FOREST RESOURCES

Like many aspects of life on Earth, forests develop and evolve through life cycles. The processes forests go through each day, week, year, decade, century, and so on, determine the development of the forest throughout time. This chapter looks at the various life cycles, resource cycles, and plant processes that occur. It then examines tree growth and its importance, as well as the adaptations forests must go through to survive the impacts they are often faced with.

FOREST DEVELOPMENT—A CRITICAL LINK IN THE CHAIN

Forests, especially the rain forests, only cover a small percentage of the Earth's surface, yet they affect the air people breathe and influence weather patterns around the world. For example, during photosynthesis, trees and other plants take in carbon dioxide (CO_2) from the air and give off the necessary oxygen that other life needs. Forests help maintain the right balance of gases in the atmosphere. They also play a major role as water buffers and reservoirs. When it rains, forests soak up water that would otherwise flow directly into rivers and out to sea. Trees take in moisture through their roots and release it later into the air as water vapor, which then forms clouds. Because forests influence weather patterns, they contribute moisture to the non-forested areas of the Earth. A major concern of scientists and other environmentalists is that if too many forests are cut down, the Earth's climate may change and become much drier.

Although trees and forests do not seem to change much from year to year, they are always changing. Trees that die are replaced by new trees. Natural disasters can occur to upset the forest balance and cause change and renewal. Trees may face many other hazards throughout their lives, such as insects, disease, drought, and pollution.

Even if trees survive these hazards, they will eventually die of old age. Just like people, as trees age, they go through several biological changes. They stop growing and producing fruit, their ability to grow new root sprouts stops, branches die and break off, and eventually they lose their strength and vitality. In this way—similar to humans—trees complete a life cycle.

A forest is renewed when new seeds germinate and sprout. Many deciduous and evergreen trees grow back from buds on their roots and stumps. This method allows them to grow rapidly because they are able to draw on a large root system full of stored food. As the forest life evolves, each species either fills its unique niche in the ecosystem or dies off.

The flow of energy is present in the animal life as well. An animal's food originally comes from the forest plants; whether the animal is an herbivore (plant-eating), omnivore (plant- and meat-eating), or carnivore (meat-eating). Sunlight is ultimately the source of this energy; green plants use sunlight to manufacture food in the process of photosynthesis.

In forests, the rate of energy flow is not steady, however. The season of the year has a major impact on the amount of activity in a forest ecosystem. For example, spring and summer are busy, productive times. In autumn, the processes slow down; in the winter, the processes shut down (it is this dormancy that causes deciduous plants to lose their leaves each fall).

Animal life slows down, too. Some animals hibernate to conserve energy, while others slow down significantly in a state of **torpor** (sleepiness), and still others (like birds) may migrate to warmer climates during the cold winter.

PLANT PROCESSES—THE FLOW OF ENERGY

Plants need water, sunshine, warmth, minerals, and gases in order to grow well and remain healthy. These elements come from the air and soil. A plant is able to produce simple sugars (glucose and sucrose) using the carbon dioxide from the air and water from the soil. In order to do this, the plant also requires the use of sunlight. Of the sunlight that strikes the plant, green plants absorb only 30%, and only 2% of this energy is stored. The plant's green leaves trap the energy from the sunlight. Chlorophyll allows the plant to make food. Plants need energy for growth, movement, transporting materials around their bodies, and to make complex chemicals.

Sunlight is what provides the power to combine carbon dioxide and water to produce sugar. This food manufacturing process is called photosynthesis. During photosynthesis, the light energy received by **chlorophyll** is trapped in the chloroplasts (the body within the plant cell that contains chlorophyll), which have received water from the veins and carbon dioxide from the air. Minerals come from the soil. They dissolve in water and enter the plant through the root system.

To stay alive, the plant's cells must break down food in order to obtain energy. This process is called **respiration**. Respiration is the opposite of photosynthesis: While photosynthesis stores energy, respiration releases it. Photosynthesis makes sugar and gives off oxygen. Respiration uses oxygen to break apart sugar. Transpiration is the process by which moisture is carried through plants, where it changes to vapor and is released into the atmosphere. In other words, transpiration is the evaporation of water from plant leaves. Plants release nearly 10% of their moisture content to the air through transpiration.

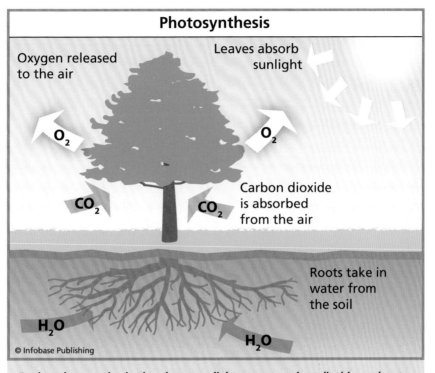

Photosynthesis

Oxygen released to the air

Leaves absorb sunlight

O_2

O_2

Carbon dioxide is absorbed from the air

CO_2

CO_2

Roots take in water from the soil

H_2O

H_2O

© Infobase Publishing

During photosynthesis, the plant uses light energy, carbon dioxide, and water to make sugars. The plant uses these sugars as an energy source.

CYCLES OF LIFE—MAINTAINING A BALANCE

There are several natural cycles in nature that support the forest. Two of the most critical cycles pertaining to forest resources are the hydrologic (water) cycle and the forest nutrient cycle.

In an ecosystem, the inorganic nutrients cycle through more than just the organisms. They also enter into the atmosphere, the oceans, the ground, and the rocks. Because chemicals cycle through the biological world (living things) and the geologic, or physical, world (the oceans, land, and atmosphere), the cycles that affect ecosystems are often referred to as *biogeochemical cycles*.

When chemicals are held in storage for long periods of time, they are said to be contained in reservoirs. When a chemical is not held in a particular place for a long time—but moves through the system faster—the chemicals are said to be in exchange pools.

The Water Cycle

Water is necessary for animal survival, plant growth, for dissolving and transporting plant nutrients, and for survival of soil organisms. The water cycle is fundamental to all living things on Earth. The endless movement and recycling of water between the atmosphere, the land's surface, and underground is called the hydrologic cycle, or water cycle.

Once water reaches the ground, it can go in several directions before it returns again to the atmosphere. Animals and plants can use the water, it can be stored in lakes, or it can seep into the soil. The sun's energy can then make the water evaporate back into the atmosphere or the Earth's gravity can pull the water that has entered the ground down through the soil to be stored for years as slowly moving groundwater, from where it can later seep into springs and resurface.

Water on the surface is returned to the atmosphere through the process of evaporation. Water that has been used by plants is returned to the atmosphere as vapor through transpiration, which happens when water passes through the leaves of plants. Forests filter stream water and absorb water to control flooding, improving the health of the soil. Evaporation from tree leaves cools and humidifies the air. Trees are such powerful water removers that the soil in the forest sometimes gets drier than soil in open fields.

The Forest Nutrient Cycle

Nutrients are simple chemicals found in the soil. The most important are nitrogen, phosphorous, and potassium. There are usually huge quantities of these elements in the soil, but they are mostly "locked up" in soil particles. These particles release their stored nutrient molecules slowly in the water that is always present within the soil. Roots pick up these nutrients.

Nitrogen comes from the air. Before it can be used by plants, it must be changed from a gas into a salt (nitrate). Some plants enrich the soil by adding large amounts of nitrogen, using microbes that live in their roots. Nitrogen is usually the nutrient that is in shortest supply.

When plants decompose, their nutrients are released back into the soil. Fortunately, only small amounts are washed out of the soil into streams. New nutrients are constantly being added from soil particles, bedrock, and other sources.

Tropical forests differ from temperate and boreal forests, as we saw in the last chapter. Because rain forest soils are thinner than temperate forest soils, rain forests immediately re-absorb and utilize the nutrient instead of storing nutrients in the soil and roots like the temperate forests.

TREE GROWTH AND DEVELOPMENT—A WINDOW TO THE PAST

A tree system is much bigger than it may seem at first glance, because half the tree (in a temperate or boreal forest) is underground, supported by extensive root systems. In fact, the roots spread out about twice as far as the longest branches. Feeder roots soak up water and nutrients near the ground's surface. Larger roots deeper down in the soil hold the tree up. The roots grow about 1 or 2 feet (0.3 to 0.6 m) per year.

The trunk holds up the treetop. The part of the trunk that grows is called the cambium (it is a thin layer of cells between the bark and the wood). The outside of the cambium layer produces bark, and the inside of the cambium makes new wood. Sugar from the leaves moves down to the roots through the inner bark, or **phloem**. As the phloem dies, it becomes bark, which protects the tree from fire, insects, and disease. Water moves up from the roots to the leaves through the sapwood, or **xylem**. Heartwood is the dead dark-colored wood in the center of the trunk.

Every year, the tree adds a layer of wood over the entire outside of the tree (including the trunk, branches, and twigs). Wood formed

By looking at the rings on a tree, it is possible to calculate its age. The light rings show the fast spring and early summer growth of the tree. The dark rings show the slower growth of late summer and early fall. Thicker rings represent wetter years; thinner rings represent drier years. Each pair of light and dark rings counts for one year of growth. By counting the rings starting at the center of the stump, the age of the tree can be calculated. *(Photo courtesy Nature's Images)*

in the spring ("spring wood") is less dense than wood formed in the summer ("summer wood"). This differential growth forms rings, called growth rings, which can be seen in a cross-section of a trunk or branch. Growth rings record the tree's history. Wide rings grow in good years when the climate is more mild and more water is available; narrow rings grow in poor years when the climate is more harsh and less water exists.

The leaves are the food manufacturers. They contain the chlorophyll to make sugar through photosynthesis. As explained previously, sugar from photosynthesis is the building block trees use to make leaves, roots, bark, and wood. In the short term, photosynthesis takes carbon dioxide out of the atmosphere and releases oxygen. Tree rings present a window to the past by allowing scientists to determine how old the tree is and what the past climate was like.

ADAPTATIONS FOR SURVIVAL

An adaptation is a special characteristic a plant or animal has to ensure its highest chances for survival in a particular ecosystem. One form of adaptation found in nature is camouflage—the ability of an organism to blend in with its surroundings. For example, many tropical bird's feathers are green to blend in with the foliage; and some insects may resemble the twigs and branches they live on. Jaguar coats often resemble the speckled ground matter's appearance so that they can lie in wait for prey without being detected.

Shape and color can hide or reveal. Many rain forest creatures depend on their unique appearance for their survival. Most forest animals need to hide—both from their predators and also from the animals they hunt. Colorings, shapes, and markings allow species to blend into the background to better survive. Adaptations do not occur overnight. Oftentimes they have evolved over lengthy periods of time. Adaptations give the life-form a better chance of surviving in its surroundings. If a life-form cannot adapt and the environment changes significantly, the species may become extinct.

Many different types of conditions can change in a forest over time, forcing plants and animals to adapt in order to survive. For example, major changes can be caused by the following:

- weather
- climatic change
- fire
- insects and disease
- forest succession (the changes that a forest naturally goes through)

Tree with spines, evolved for defense. Many rain forest plants like this palm protect themselves from predators with physical defenses like spines. *(Photo by Rhett Butler, Mongabay.com)*

- interactions of plants and animals (competition for water, space, sunlight, and shelter)
- humans (humans have had the greatest effect of all. This includes the introduction of diseases, clearing and farming lands, and the use of destructive timber-cutting methods.)

Furcifer pardalis chameleon in Maroantsetra, Madagascar. This male chameleon is showing breeding coloration. *(Photo by Rhett Butler, Mongabay.com)*

Some forests are more resilient than others. The more resilient, the better able they are to recover from the impacts listed above. Species that are not resilient will die out. Adaptations are especially critical in the rain forest because of the intense competition—species must adapt to fit a narrow, specific niche in the system if they are to survive. For instance, if they are to survive growing on the forest floor, they must be able to compensate for the lack of direct sunlight. Many flowers have evolved specific structures that help ensure **pollination** by the insects they attract. Many leaves in the rain forest are specially designed to repel the rainwater that falls on them by growing a waxy covering and a pointed "drip tip" that allow rainwater and fallen seeds to run off. The buttress roots, discussed earlier, are another good example of adaptation.

Many plants have developed specific defenses, such as tough leaves, thick bark, sharp spines, and stinging hairs. Some plants trap insects by producing poisonous chemical substances. Other plants use a chemical means of defense. They produce chemicals that are harmless while inside the leaf, but poisonous if released and exposed to the sunlight.

Other flowers are brightly colored to entice pollination by insects and birds. Some species shed all their leaves, just leaving the flowers on the branches so they will be easily noticed. Some flowers have a petal that will only support an insect of a certain weight. Other flowers only open at night because they need to be pollinated by a specific species of bat.

Some organisms adapt to specific climatic conditions, others to eat a certain type of food, while others have adapted to avoid being eaten by specific predators. Most animals have behavioral adaptations, which help them attract a mate. Monkeys that live in the rain forest canopy have arms, legs, and tails that are adapted for swinging from branch to branch. Parrots have developed specialized feet with two curling front toes and two curling back toes to help them hold onto branches.

Adaptations are always evolving as the forest ecosystem changes. As one species changes, others must in turn adapt, similar to a row of dominoes. This process continues in cycles. Once an adaptation has been successfully made, new conditions can trigger another change, starting the process all over again.

CHAPTER 5

USES OF FORESTS AND THE RESULTING IMPACTS

This chapter examines the use of forests and the resulting impacts on them. There are many impacts that forests face today, such as urbanization, erosion, fire, pollution, deforestation, overexploitation, loss of biodiversity, climate change, introduction of invasive species, logging, and recreation. Without proper management and **conservation**, one or a combination of these impacts can threaten the future health of forests.

LANDS OF MANY USES

As the previous chapters have illustrated, forests are much more than simply trees. They are complex interrelated communities of trees, shrubs, herbs, flowers, fungi, bacteria, and a broad variety of wildlife. In the United States, some forests are owned by the individual states, some are privately owned, and some are managed by the federal government and owned by all the citizens of the United States (these lands are referred to as *public domain*). The U.S. Forest Service manages 156 forests across the United States.

These lands are used by the public for many purposes, such as camping, fishing, hiking, backpacking, mountain biking, wildlife watching, snowmobiling, cross-country skiing, downhill skiing, snowshoeing, timber resources, cattle grazing, and mineral extraction. Because of all these uses, the forestlands must be managed very carefully in order to keep the land pristine and healthy. Oftentimes, this is a balancing act as different uses can conflict with each other. In addition, if some of the uses become extreme, it can damage the entire ecosystem. Fortunately, the national forests in the United States are well-managed and able to support the uses found on them. If a current use in a national forest becomes a problem to the ecosystem, the multiple-use policies for that forest are adjusted to fit the needs of the environment.

Forest land in other developed countries, such as Western Europe, Canada, Australia, and New Zealand, is also well-managed and environmentally sound. Today, the forests under the biggest threat are those found in the developing countries—where most of the world's rain forests are located.

THREATS TO THE FORESTS

Forests worldwide face a variety of threats. Some result from forces of nature, such as floods, drought, and wildfire; but the most common (and preventable) threats to forests are caused by people. The rain forests are especially hard hit. The ever-expanding human population is exerting tremendous pressure on the resources and the space of the rain forest.

Urbanization

Natural ecosystems are often most seriously affected by urban development. When developers build shopping centers, housing developments, office buildings, gas stations, and other structures, critical habitat is not just degraded, it is often destroyed. Urban sprawl can also threaten species to the point of endangerment or extinction. If a species habitat is taken by humans and converted to another use, and if the species cannot adapt to these changes, it will die.

Historically, urbanization has had an impact on the temperate forests of the United States. Many of these forests were cut down by new settlers. Today, only about 3% of the original temperate forests in the United States remains intact. According to the National Park Service, one example of the impact of urbanization on temperate forests is Olympic National Park in Washington State. Before the arrival of homesteaders (people settling land and building homes and communities) a hundred years ago, the Olympic Peninsula contained more than a million acres of old-growth spruce and hemlock. Because of unchecked habitat destruction, many plants and animals have had their habitat reduced to a few lone "islands" inside the forest. Fortunately, in the United States, these consequences of urbanization have been recognized and corrected. Management plans have been put in place to protect these habitats.

As human populations increase in tropical regions, people are moving away from the crowded cities to the forests instead where they build homes and practice small-scale farming. Commercial large-scale agricultural projects are also being developed, which require conversion of large plots of rain forest. These changes can harm the soil, lower the productivity, and permanently destroy the land's resources.

According to Conservation International, the coastal forests of eastern Africa—Somalia, Kenya, Tanzania, and Mozambique—are facing serious loss of forests because of urbanization and agricultural conversion of the rain forests. Today, only about 10% of the original vegetation (11,256 square miles, or 29,125 sq. km) remains in pristine condition. The remaining habitat is limited to more than 400 patches of lowland forest, covering about 2,416 square miles (6,259 sq. km).

The expansion of agriculture presents the most significant threat, because the soil is poor and can only support subsistence agriculture (only growing what the farmer needs for himself, not for trade). Most short-term shifting cultivation concentrates on food crops such as maize (corn), banana, and coconut. As the human population is increasing 2.5% to 3.5% each year, the demand for additional farmland is also increasing. By creating plantations that raise just a few select crops, the natural ecosystems are being destroyed.

The burning of woody plants for charcoal production also causes major habitat loss. Forests close to tourist areas suffer from the high demand for carving wood and timber for the construction of hotels, private residences, and tourist attractions. The illegal poaching of carving wood trees has also put those forests in jeopardy.

Uncontrolled burning to clear farmland, to drive animals for hunting, to collect honey, and to reduce tsetse flies also threatens the lowland coastal forests. In some of these areas, the natural species are replaced by the more common fire-adapted species.

Some people try to graze cattle and other livestock in rain forest areas in order to capitalize on the huge worldwide demand for beef. Unfortunately, when the rain forests are cleared, grazing can only occur for a short period of time before the nutrients in the soil are used up and nothing grows. This has become a significant problem in countries such as Brazil in the Amazon. According to the Center for International Forestry Research, the rate of forest destruction is currently 6.7 million acres (2.5 million hectares) each year. In just ten years time (1990–2000) an area of land the size of the country of Portugal was deforested.

Cattle expansion in the Amazon in the last decade has been staggering. During this period, the number of cattle more than doubled, from 26 million in 1990 to 57 million in 2002. As the demand in the Western world for cheap meat increases, more and more rain forests are destroyed to provide grazing land. Today, there are an estimated 220 million head of cattle, 20 million goats, 60 million pigs, and 700 million chickens on the rain forest farms. To graze one steer in the Amazon rain forest requires two acres of land.

Erosion

Soil erosion often results from removing the natural vegetation on forested lands (trees act as a stabilizer of the soil). Without trees to offer the soil protection, the rain has enormous erosive potential. Each rainstorm can remove soil and nutrients from the ground. Another

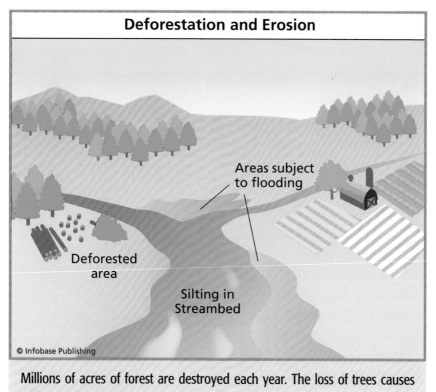

Deforestation and Erosion

Areas subject to flooding

Deforested area

Silting in Streambed

© Infobase Publishing

Millions of acres of forest are destroyed each year. The loss of trees causes widespread erosion.

problem is that excessive erosion not only degrades the landscape and ecosystem, it can trigger landslides. Steep, clear-cut slopes are the most vulnerable areas for landslide destruction.

Erosion has a negative effect on future vegetation in the area. When the topsoil becomes eroded, it is very difficult for new plants to grow. It creates a vicious cycle, because without the stabilizing effect of roots in the soil, the rate of erosion increases. Once erosion begins, it is extremely difficult to control.

Erosion also has a serious impact on streams and the life within them. Fish and other freshwater animals need clear water to survive. When erosion occurs on the land's surface, the washed-away soil, carried by the rain, ends up being emptied into the rivers. Because wildlife (such as salmon) needs fresh water in order to survive, polluting their habitat is deadly to them.

Fire

Fire is one of the natural disturbances that forests have evolved to cope with over time. Fires caused by lightning strikes have shaped and altered forests for millions of years. Some forest trees actually require fire in order to spread their seeds. Although these natural fires are common to a forest's environment, the increase in human encroachment on forested lands has caused an increase in human-induced forest fires.

Forest fires move in unpredictable ways under the influence of wind patterns, weather, ground material, presence of dry vegetation, and topography. Some fires—called crown fires—can leap from treetop to treetop, quickly igniting a large area of forest. Ground fires can creep through the duff (loose organic matter on the ground), and fires may smolder below the surface for long periods of time.

In the past, forest managers sought to prevent fires through public education and close monitoring of the forests. They believed the best course of action to keep a forest healthy was to prevent forest fires. When fires would occur, they would be suppressed as quickly as possible. The problem with this approach, however, was that it actually increased the wildfire potential in an area. Because trees that had died were not removed, over time all the organic matter from trees collected on the forest floor, becoming very dry and prone to burn hot when a fire was triggered either naturally or by humans. If a fire was eventually triggered, the debris transformed into huge amounts of "forest fuel," which increased the severity, danger, and damage of the fire.

Fortunately, land management practices have evolved as foresters better understand the mechanisms of forests. The relationship between forests, fires, insects, disease, and climate are only recently beginning to be understood.

The huge fires in 1988 that burned more than 1.5 million acres (567,000 hectares) of land in Yellowstone National Park is part of what has brought on a new philosophy of **forest management**. It was one

Due to the variable conditions of dryness, temperature, wind speed, and type of vegetation, fires can sweep unpredictably through an area. *(Courtesy Bureau of Land Management, photo by Kelly Rigby)*

of the worst wildfires in U.S. history. For months prior to the fires, the weather had been hot and dry. As a result, lightning started more than 45 fires. Other fires were started by careless people. Strong winds spread the fires. Pine forests that had grown for hundreds of years were destroyed in minutes.

Firefighters from all over the country worked hard day and night, trying to get the fire under control. Unfortunately, they could not put it out completely. Finally, in September, the moist fall weather set in. Snowfall eventually extinguished the fire.

Several factors influence the way fires behave and move. Wind can make fires unpredictable, which can cause the flames to turn and surround firefighters. Steep slopes can influence the movement of air, causing warm air to rise up the slope, spreading the fire uphill during the day. At night, the wind can change direction and flow downhill. This shifting of wind direction must be taken into account when placing fire fighters in the area in order to keep them safe.

Suppression (actually fighting a fire) can be done in many ways, depending on the rate of spread and the intensity of the fire. A ground fire can be contained by digging dirt trenches surrounding it, removing it from other fuels (burnable vegetation), and using backpack water pumps. In inaccessible areas, firefighters call in aerial water and fire retardant bombers (planes). Crown fires are very dangerous and are usually fought from a distance. Fire-retardant chemicals may be sprayed on buildings in a fire's path. Fighting fires is expensive. According to John E. Larsen, a fire fighter for the U.S. Bureau of Land Management, each load of fire retardant dropped by an airplane over the fire costs approximately $5,000. Fighting fires costs millions of dollars each year.

Forest managers have learned a lot from experience. Today, fires are often set intentionally in a process called a "controlled burn." This serves to get rid of the excess dead organic matter in an area, effectively removing part of the fire fuel potential from the land, so that if lightning strikes, the destruction from a fire would not be as severe. Scientists also believe the smoke released in huge fires contributes to **global warming** and climate change.

Helicopters assist in battling fires. This helicopter carries a container filled with water and transports it to the fire, where it is dropped. Precision and timing are critical. Wind conditions and poor visibility due to excess smoke can make this operation tricky. *(Courtesy Bureau of Land Management, photo by Kelly Rigby)*

Forest fires can have many consequences. Vegetation is destroyed, beneficial soil organisms may be killed, and trees can take a long time to recover. In addition, when animal habitat is destroyed they are left with no food or shelter and must find a new territory.

Pollution

Air pollution has a negative effect on the health of forests. When pollution enters the air from gasoline and diesel used in cars, fossil-fuel-fired electric power plants, industrial boilers, and home furnaces, it mixes with the moisture in the atmosphere. Some of the most hard-hit areas are the mountaintop trees, which are smothered in harmful acidic fogs and also experience high ozone levels. When it rains, these acids are redeposited back on Earth—a phenomena called acid rain.

The pollutants enter the tissues of living organisms and are then passed up through the food chain, where they increase in toxicity—a process called *bioaccumulation*. Acid rain harms forests in several ways. When it lands on a tree's leaves, it erodes their protective coating and makes them vulnerable to insects. When the leaves harmed by acid rain fall to the forest floor, they do not decompose very fast because the acid kills the organisms in the soil that are necessary to decompose the organic matter, causing an accumulation of ammonia in the soil. The effects of pollution keep new forest growth from developing by killing the seedlings in the area. Acid rain also physically damages the tree's roots, decreasing the rate of growth, and eventually killing the tree.

Acid rain also affects the area's water. When acid rain from industrial gases falls on forests, the rain can be 10 or 20 times as acidic as unpolluted rain. Once the rain reaches the ground, the soil, lakes, and ponds also become acidic.

Unfortunately, this is a common scenario. In the developed areas of the world, serious acid rain problems have occurred from industrial emissions in the eastern United States, eastern Canada, and Eastern Europe. Even worse, the pollutants can be carried great distances by prevailing winds. Because this has become such a serious problem, the United States, along with 24 other countries, has agreed to keep nitrogen oxide levels at 1987 levels as part of the Long-Range Transboundary Air Pollution Agreement. The Clean Air Act was enacted to cut the sulfur dioxide emissions from power plants.

Logging—Overcutting and Exploitation

Although people have cut down forests since ancient times, it has only been in the last few hundred years that the rates have rapidly increased and the consequences are becoming better understood. For example, much of the natural forests were cut down when settlers arrived in the United States in the 1700s and 1800s. Thick, natural forested areas on the East Coast rapidly disappeared. Today, massive deforestation is now occurring in the Amazon rain forest.

Overcutting threatens forest health in many ways. Widespread cutting—called **clear-cutting**—creates forest **fragmentation** and leads to a loss of biodiversity because it destroys key habitats. Erosion is a problem when the vegetation is removed and the soil is left unprotected. It takes centuries to build the soil—considered a nonrenewable resource—back up, and oftentimes, the area loses its diversity and becomes unproductive.

In the 1800s, the redwood forests of the United States were seriously overcut. Valued for their large wood content, redwood forests have been used by humans for centuries to build homes, canoes, and other items. During this time period, large-scale logging of the redwood forests occurred. As technology advanced, clear cutting increased.

Then the massive deforestation in American forests moved inland. In the early 1900s, about 500 million board feet of redwoods were harvested each year. Then, from 1947 to 1958, this rate rose to a billion board feet each year. Sadly, today much of America's old growth forests have been cut down. What remains is now protected by effective forest management practices. Most of the redwoods cut today are second-growth trees.

Another impact from logging is the construction of access roads. These roads disturb the ecosystem and lead to erosion. In addition, if trees are removed in isolated clusters, it harms wildlife habitat and forces animals into smaller and smaller pockets of isolated space.

Common Agents of Deforestation

Agents	Method of deforestation
Slash-and-burn farmers	Clear forest to grow subsistence and cash crops.
Commercial farmers	Clear the forest to plant commercial cash crops. They sometimes run slash-and-burn farmers out.
Livestock herders	Herding animals can ruin the soil.
Cattle ranchers	They clear the forest to plant grasses, which ultimately, the rain forest cannot support.
Commercial tree planters	These groups clear the leftover forest debris from previously logged forests to sell to the pulp and paper industries.
Loggers	They remove large-scale commercial timber. They also impact the environment by constructing roads.
Land settlement planners	They are involved in the relocation of people into forested areas, often displacing the local residents.
Firewood collectors	They remove important biomass from the forests.
Mining and petroleum industrialists	They work in localized areas and clear the forest for road construction and to haul in equipment.

(Source: Food and Agriculture Organization of the United Nations)

This is an example of a logging method known as clear-cutting. In clear-cutting, all the trees are taken from a specific area. With select cutting, only certain trees are taken from an area, thereby leaving some habitat remaining. This logging was done in an area containing northern spotted owls in Oregon. *(Courtesy U.S. Fish and Wildlife Service)*

Clear cutting also disturbs the natural succession of species. Many resource managers support a new approach called "selective logging," which is the practice of taking only certain trees from an area rather than completely clearing it.

Some managers have proposed clear-cut areas be replanted with one specific tree (called monoculture). Others argue that reintroducing only one species negatively impacts the entire ecosystem of plants and animals that had traditionally existed in the area. Others believe that the so-called tree plantations do not produce as high a quality product—old trees produce stronger wood with larger fibers than young plantation trees. Forests that are clear-cut also eliminate other possible activities, such as tourism.

Logging in the rain forest for timber has increased in recent years. Many rain forest trees contain valuable hardwoods, such as teak and mahogany woods that command a high price. These woods are popular in the construction of furniture, floors, and custom homes. But hardwood trees grow very slowly, and cannot be replaced quickly (making them largely nonrenewable). Because this wood is valuable as carving wood, poaching (stealing) timber has become a huge problem in many rain forest areas.

Another threat to rain forest areas is the practice of slash-and-burn where vegetation is removed and the area is burned. Once the trees are cleared out and burned, it leaves the soil bare and susceptible to erosion because nothing exists to bind and stabilize the soil.

Other forests are clear cut in order to manufacture paper. Experts believe that by the year 2050, more than 3 billion trees will be cut down and processed just to keep up with the world's need for toilet paper.

Other areas are cleared and built into terraces to grow rice. All over Southeast Asia, rain forest has been cut down to make way for rice paddies. Although terraces have been built for centuries, the rapid increase of this practice today due to growing populations has become much more destructive.

Loss of Biodiversity

Biodiversity and the habitats that exist today on Earth have taken millions of years to develop. When species are threatened and become extinct, it can take millions of years for new species to evolve in their place. Although natural extinctions have occurred throughout time (such as the dinosaurs, woolly mammoths, and saber-toothed tigers), recent human activity has had a far bigger impact on species. Because humans are involved in activities such as clear cutting, farming, ranching, and urbanization, many scientists fear that up to 20% of all the species that exist on Earth today could be threatened, endangered, or extinct 15 years from now.

An uncut rain forest has multiple layers of thick, dense undergrowth and multiple canopies above it. The biodiversity is so rich that hundreds of species exist in a small area. *(Photo courtesy Nature's Images)*

The loss of even one species can ruin a forest ecosystem. In addition, the loss of plant species means the loss of unknown economic potential—humans will never know if a particular plant that has been destroyed would have been valuable for food crops, fibers, medicines, or other useful products. For example, there could well be a medicinal cure for cancer, AIDS, or other serious diseases that may never be discovered and used to benefit humans, because it was destroyed first.

Another major impact is that species in the rain forest are so diverse and adapted to a small, specific habitat, that if that habitat is destroyed, the impacted species will have nowhere else to go, and so it is destroyed along with its habitat.

Climate Change

Forests help prevent global warming. The leaves on forest trees release water vapor, which helps keep the forest and nearby areas cool. When trees are cleared from the forest, fewer trees are available to go through the process of photosynthesis. This leaves more carbon dioxide than usual in the atmosphere (trees are a natural "carbon sink," storing large amounts of carbon dioxide). The result is that less of the sun's heat is reflected back into space by water vapor. Instead, the heat from the sun is trapped near the surface of the Earth by carbon dioxide and other gases.

Experts believe that the effect of this trapped heat—a phenomena called the *greenhouse effect*—is contributing to the steady warming of the Earth's climate. There is a natural greenhouse effect—which is what keeps our planet warm enough to be inhabitable—but the greenhouse effect this is referring to is the artificial one caused by humans. This greenhouse effect is caused by pollution, such as that from burning fossil fuels in cars. Scientists fear that Earth's increasing temperatures may eventually lead to devastating weather conditions, such as large-scale flooding from melting ice caps and rising sea levels.

To help prevent global warming caused by the greenhouse effect, some scientists have suggested planting new trees in forests when others are cut down or burned. Another option scientists have suggested is that fewer trees be cut down or burned in the future. Burning forests is undesirable because burning wood releases additional carbon dioxide into the atmosphere (the CO_2 that was stored in the tree). Other specialists believe that the current depletion of the ozone layer increases the Earth to the exposure of more ultraviolet radiation from the sun, which adversely affects plants and animals.

On a broader scale, it is true that climate is always changing. Normally, natural fluctuations are so gradual that oftentimes trees can migrate to new areas that provide better habitat for survival, but this gradual migration of species to more desirable areas can take thousands of years. Because of the interference of human activities, however, some scientists expect the climate to change more quickly. If it happens too fast, forests may die off because the altered climate does not allow time for the spread of seeds to a better ecological location.

Mining

Mining is another activity that can be destructive to forests. Mining for gold, bauxite (from which aluminum is made), and other minerals can lead to widespread destruction of the land. Mining for commodities such as coal, granite, and other resources involves removing the forest trees to get to the rock underneath. Often, acids and chemicals contaminate the soils. Many areas of mining lands become damaged to the extent that forests do not grow again on the depleted soils. And, like clear cutting, once the land has been disturbed by mining efforts, it becomes vulnerable to erosion.

One case in point is the coastal forests of eastern Africa. They have suffered a lot of destruction because of their rich mineral resources—gas, gemstones, iron, titanium, limestone, and kaolin. Unfortunately, destructive mining practices can destroy large areas of natural habitat. High-grade silica sands for glass manufacture are mined in Africa, as well as iron and manganese. There are also extensive areas of limestone along the coast, as well as rubies and other precious stones; mining of these resources destroys the health of the forests through overexploitation and destruction.

Recreation

Some outdoor recreational activities can be harmful to forests. For example, off-road vehicles (OHVs) such as motorbikes and four-wheelers can be a threat to forest areas, especially when ridden off designated trails. Motorized vehicles like these tear up fragile plants, scare wildlife, crush animal burrows, and increase erosion. They also spoil the solitude that many forested areas offer.

How You Can Help Save Endangered Trees

You can help protect the trees in the area where you live by following some simple guidelines:

- Plant new trees whenever possible. Trees provide shelter for wildlife and help the environment, add oxygen to the air, and help alleviate global warming.
- Always try to recycle products made from paper and cardboard. For every ton of recycled paper that is made, 17 trees are saved.
- Always buy recycled paper products rather than new paper ones. It also uses less energy to create a product made from recycled material than it does a new one.
- Even though they are convenient, avoid using disposable plates, napkins, cups, and other similar paper products.
- Choose products with little or no packaging. Product packaging (such as boxes and wrappers) uses a lot of paper products. A lot of energy is also wasted to manufacture packaging materials, because these items can only be used once.
- Recycle newspapers, writing paper, computer paper, and cardboard. Start collecting these types of products, and you will be surprised how quickly they accumulate—a visual example of how many disposable wood products we use each day.

Deforestation in Madagascar leaves hillsides vulnerable to erosion. *(Photo by Rhett Butler, Mongabay.com)*

Deforestation

The end result of all of the previously listed impacts is deforestation. Deforestation—whether deliberate or unintended—is the result of the removal of trees without reforestation. It can be caused by many things, such as the deliberate removal of forest for agricultural or urban development, uncontrolled grazing, mining, or the acquisition of timber. In the rain forests of developing countries, the rate of deforestation is reaching new highs each year.

The issues surrounding deforestation that natural resource managers face are important ones. If good management and conservation practices are not put in place now, then continued deforestation will lead to a series of ecological problems that will affect people, animals, and plants—even outside of the forest environment. If large areas of forest are destroyed, soil will erode and heavy rainfalls will trigger flooding. Making wise critical management decisions now will provide everyone with forests tomorrow.

CHAPTER 6

THE IMPORTANCE OF FOREST RESOURCES

Forests play an extremely important role in peoples' lives world-wide—from food to medicines to many other useful products. This chapter examines the importance of the goods and services people receive from forests, the critical sources of medicine they provide, the concept of bioprospecting, the contributions of urban forests, and the benefits of tourism associated with forests.

GOODS AND SERVICES

The rain forests of the world are a tremendous resource providing a major storehouse of things such as fruits, vegetables, ingredients for medicines, and construction materials. Scientists believe that what has already been discovered is just a small piece of the pie—that there are many species of plants and animals in the rain forests that have not even been discovered yet.

As illustrated previously, rain forests are disappearing at record rates, mainly because some of the resources that come from them (such as

Elephants are often used for transportation in Indonesia. The riders on these elephants are tourists doing a rain forest tour in Java, Indonesia. *(Photo by Rhett Butler, Mongabay.com)*

lumber, oil, and gold) are not sustainably harvested, only using as much as can be replenished. Sadly, future human and animal generations will not be able to benefit from the rain forest's resources if this continues.

There are many goods and services that result from forests, including both tangible and intangible varieties. Tangible items are objects that can be picked up and physically felt. These are the plants that people trade, buy, and sell. Tangible plant goods include sugar, bananas, nuts, coffee, rubber, and many more commodities.

Tangible services include employment opportunities in many types of businesses, which provide jobs for scientists, farmers, building suppliers, chemists, biologists, ecologists, land planners, land managers, pharmacologists, and many more.

There are also intangible goods and services associated with forests. These are the things that cannot be touched. It is sometimes hard to put a value on some of the intangible goods and services because they are priceless. Intangible items include the addition of oxygen to the atmosphere for all life to breathe (the foundation of food webs), habitat for wildlife, biodiversity, recreational opportunities, scenic landscapes, and natural beauty to look at and enjoy. In addition, forests store approximately 800 gigatons (a gigaton is equal to one billion tons) of carbon, which makes them an important natural defense against climate change. They also provide water infiltration and clean water as a service to millions of people.

Food and Other Products

Since recorded time, humans have relied on tropical forests. Jungle areas of the world have provided people with a steady supply of woods, plants, and animals and have supplied fruits, fibers, grains, clothes, resins, medicine, pigments, and many other materials. Agrarian and hunter-gatherer lifestyles depended on forests. Historically, major trade routes were developed to accommodate forest resources.

Today, although many people—especially in the United States—live far from the rain forests, most people fail to recognize that the distant rain forests provide a global food supply by offering new, disease-resistant crops; billions of dollars worth of trade in tropical timber; nontimber forest products; a stable and livable climate for the entire world; regular rain; and clean air.

Almost half of today's main food crops were originally discovered in their natural state in the rain forest. Plants that originated, or still live, in the forests provide people with fruits, nuts, and grains, such as ginger, nutmeg, peppercorn, peppers, oranges, pineapples, avocados, bananas, guava, papayas, mangoes, tea, sugar, rice, maize (corn), cashews, peanuts, yams, coconuts, cloves, vanilla, cinnamon, coffee, and even chocolate.

Forests contain tremendous potential. Agricultural research is an especially important area affected by the rain forests. New crops are cultivated from forest species, and genetic material from wild plants can be used to improve harvests from existing crops. Many food and other product resources first originated as wild plants. Today, many of them have been cultivated for the world market on large plantations. Although these plantations take some of the stress off of the wild vegetation, it still impacts the rain forests when forests are cleared to make way for commercial plantations.

The Amazon and other rain forests have had a major impact on the food that is eaten by people all over the world. For example, the banana plant—which was once restricted to certain areas of forest—is now grown throughout the tropics from the Caribbean Islands and Amazon rain forest to Africa. The global rain forest food economy is worth billions of dollars to business each year.

In the Amazon, thousands of tons of commercial nuts, cashew nuts, and macadamia nuts are produced and sold. Huge plantations have been set up for large-scale production of coffee. Kola nuts are used to make cola drinks. The sapodilla, or chicle, tree produces a milky sap that thickens when heated. Chicle, the original base for chewing gum, comes from the latex (sap) of a tree that occurs from southern Mexico to northern Brazil. Flavoring and sugar are added to the sap to give it a specific flavor. The Aztecs chewed gum from the chicle tree centuries ago. The gum popular in the United States also originally came from the rain forest chicle tree—in fact, the gum with the brand name Chicklets earned its name from the rain forest tree that produces it. Today, synthetic gums have been developed in order to conserve the chicle tree resource. That is one of the benefits of analyzing rain forest products chemically. Once a chemist determines the composition of a substance, often (but not always) synthetic ingredients can be substituted for large-scale manufacture of the substance. This is common in the pharmaceutical industry.

Bananas are a food crop grown in abundance in the rain forests. *(Photo courtesy Nature's Images)*

Most sugar is made from sugarcane, a giant tropical grass. Today, sugar is grown on plantations all over the world. Cassava, another plant, is native to Mexico, Guatemala, and northern Brazil, but is now grown throughout the tropics. Cassava is a food staple used in a similar way to potatoes. They can be boiled and eaten or processed into a bread-like substance. Like potatoes, millions of people eat cassava as a main food.

Cacao is the plant that chocolate comes from. These ripe cacao pods are in Sulawesi, Indonesia. *(Photo by Rhett Butler, Mongabay.com)*

Nutmeg and allspice also come from the rain forest. Cacao comes from the eastern Andes. It was considered a "food of the gods" by the ancient Mayans and Aztecs, who made a drink from cacao seeds. Later, when the Europeans added sugar and milk to the cacao seed they invented the chocolate we enjoy today.

Vanilla is an orchid from the rain forest. Besides a flower, it is also a popular food flavoring. Once the orchid is pollinated, a bean is produced. Vanilla flavoring comes from the bean.

All seeds are important food sources for animals and birds. Because fruits and trees contain seeds, their bright colors are meant to attract the animals that eat the seeds, thereby ensuring that they are dispersed over wide areas so that more fruits and trees will grow. Nuts from the rain forest are used in things like breakfast cereals. Fruits in the rain forest are available yearlong. Fruit makes up more than half of the diet of many species of tropical birds, mammals, reptiles, insects, and even some fish.

Forests in the temperate areas, such as dogwoods and magnolias, produce fruit for migrating songbirds, which are attracted to these fruits. Because these fruits have such a high fat content, they help supply the birds with enough nutrition for their long flight south during the winter. Also, in the temperate forests, seeds and nuts are an even more important food source than fruit to many animals. These animals—such as squirrels and chipmunks—store nuts to use as a food source during the long, cold winter. Sometimes the squirrels forget where the nuts are and leave them. Some of these seeds eventually germinate and grow into trees. The table below lists examples of the different food resources found in the tropics.

Food Resources of the Tropics

Fruits	Plantain	Banana	Citrus
	Avocado	Guava	Jackfruit
	Mango	Papaya	Passion Fruit
	Pineapple	Tomato	
Vegetables	Bamboo	Eggplant	Peppers
	Winged bean		
Nuts	Brazil nut	Cashew	
Oils	Coconut	Oil palm	
Spices and flavorings	Allspice	Black pepper	Cinnamon
	Cacao	Cloves	Coffee
	Ginger	Cola	Nutmeg and mace
	Tamarind	Sugarcane	Turmeric
	Vanilla		
Starches and roots	Cassava	Rice	Sweet potato
	Water chestnut	Yam	Taro

(Source: Missouri Botanical Garden, Education Division)

In the future, as they are discovered, there will be other foods available from the rain forest. The indigenous people eat many foods from the rain forest that developed countries have not discovered yet.

Other Economic Goods

Every day, humans use products derived from forest plants. Oils, resins, waxes, gums, rubber, and other substances all come from trees.

Wood is one of the most important plant products available today; it has been used for centuries as a building material. Different types of forests provide a variety of different woods. The boreal forests supply pine, fir, and spruce (conifers). Temperate forests produce oaks and beeches (deciduous), and the most valuable hardwoods—such as teak and mahogany—grow in the world's tropical forests. The majority of timber is processed into boards or pulp for paper.

Coniferous forests produce the most timber per acre, and have the preferred trees for making pulp because their wood is composed of long fibers. Many of the major lumber companies in the United States are located in the Pacific Northwest—the area with abundant forested land. This wood is also used in building materials. Besides solid wood, wood materials are also used to make chipboard, laminated board, and plywood. These products are made by gluing together several thin strips of wood (known as veneer). They are used in construction and to make furniture.

Different types of wood work best for certain types of products. For instance, one species of willow is used to make cricket bats because it has the right weight and strength. Some woods make good musical instruments; other high-density woods produce good xylophone keys because they create a desirable musical note. Light density woods are used in interior construction because they absorb noise and make rooms quieter. Because wood is a poor conductor of heat (unlike metal), wood is often used to make the handles on pots, pans, spatulas, fire pokers, and other goods that are exposed to high levels of direct heat. Log homes are known for their ability to modify the air temperature by keeping interior heat inside, making them more energy efficient than other types of building structures. Products, such as rubber, hardwoods, essential oils, fibers, resins, dyes, and materials used in industry also come from the rain forest.

Bamboo is a member of the grass family that grows rapidly—many inches per month. It is grown throughout the tropics and used as a material source for construction and weaving. Because of its great strength, many countries use it for scaffolding when constructing tall buildings instead of the metal scaffolding that is common in the United States. It is also used for building houses, weaving baskets, building furniture, and making musical instruments.

Rubber is a valuable product obtained from the rain forest. Rubber comes from a tree in the spurge family. The raw material for natural rubber is a milk-white sap called latex. It is found just beneath the bark of the rubber tree—a tree native to the Amazon. The tree releases the latex when it is cut. This is an adaptation to ensure the rubber tree's survival. The latex is poisonous to insects, which keeps the insects from harming the tree. People have used rubber in products since the 1800s. Originally from the Brazilian Amazon, it is currently harvested on plantations in Southeast Asia. Rubber is used in a multitude of products every day.

Once the latex is collected, it is mixed with water and heated over a fire. This process produces a ball of rubber that is ready for processing. Today, however, with the high demand for rubber, natural rubber is only used for specialized uses. The bulk of rubber manufactured today for the developed world is produced from synthetic sources, thereby conserving natural sources.

Ebony is a beautiful hardwood tree native to West Africa. The wood from this tree is extremely hard and is used to make piano keys, cutlery handles, carvings, and musical instruments.

Rattan is another rain forest product. It is a fiber harvested from the liana vines that grow in the rain forest. It is used to weave baskets and make furniture. Jute is another fiber product made from rain forest plants. It is woven into burlap and used to make rope, hammocks, bags, and many other useful items. The kapok tree grows cotton-like seeds used for stuffing toys, pillows, and mattresses. Waxes from the Brazilian

Bamboo, a type of rapidly growing grass, is used to make scaffolding, furniture, housing, and many other items. This is a stand of giant bamboo (*Dendrocalamus giganteus*) on the Indonesian island of Sulawesi. *(Photo by Rhett Butler, Mongabay.com)*

wax palm are used to make lipstick. Natural dyes, aromatic oils, and perfumes are also produced from rain forest plants.

People that live in the rain forest often build and furnish their homes from plant products because they are convenient and readily accessible. Walls are made of split palm stems, and thatch for walls and roofs is made from palm leaves. The inside is furnished with baskets and mats made from vines, leaves, and canes, as well as fibers stripped from palms.

RAIN FORESTS—PHARMACY TO THE WORLD

Scientists and other experts believe the diversity of the rain forest is extremely valuable to humans. Because the rain forest has so many species interacting with each other in so many ways, biologists view it as a priceless resource of information on how life-forms and ecological systems work. Besides food and other economic goods, the rain forests are also a rich source of medicine. Because they support millions of plant, animal, and insect species they contain a multitude of chemicals. Along with this, scientists have discovered that the world's tropical forests host a huge preserve of raw materials useful in modern medicine. Plants alone offer many types of analgesics (pain killers), antibiotics, heart drugs, tranquilizing drugs, laxatives, anticoagulants, and a host of other substances.

Many of the drugs and medicines used today come from the rain forest. For example, drugs like quinine, muscle relaxants, steroids, and cancer drugs are found there. Researchers also believe there are many new drugs still awaiting discovery. Many scientists are hopeful that the cures for cancer, Alzheimer's disease, diabetes, muscular dystrophy, and AIDS will one day be found in the rain forest and developed into revolutionary new medical cures.

The reason why the rain forests host such a rich reserve of medicinal plants is due to the adaptation of plants and animals there. As we saw in previous chapters, because the rain forest is home to so many diverse species, each species is confined to a fairly small area. When there are high concentrations, species have to compete against each other for food, light, and living space. In order to deal with this competition and survive, many species have developed forms of "biological warfare." In order to fight the competition, tropical forest species have developed special defenses to ensure their survival, such as unique biocompounds (such as poisons) in the organisms' tissues that they use for defense, attack, and survival. These processes have evolved over millions of years, which is another reason why disturbing the ecosystems can have disastrous consequences.

There are many plants known to the indigenous people (such as shamans or medicine men) whose secrets are still to be discovered by the developed world. Evidence of the U.S. government's and private pharmaceutical companies' interest is demonstrated by the multitude of ongoing research projects that are geared to learn more about the specific plants that are being used by traditional medicine men for healing, survival, and well being.

Many experts recognize that extracting these secrets will be a long, ongoing process, and they are concerned that the rain forest may be wiped out before the secrets can be learned. Because of the already rapid rate of destruction, they fear certain important cures for serious illnesses have already been destroyed before they were discovered.

In northwestern Amazonia, forest-dwelling Indians use about 1,300 plant species for medicines. In Southeast Asia, traditional healers use about 6,500 plants in treatments for malaria, stomach ulcers, syphilis, and other disorders.

Use of traditional medicines is widespread throughout the developing world. Almost 90% of the people in developing countries still rely on traditional medicine, based on different species of plants and animals in the rain forest, for their primary health care. In the United States, one-fourth of the prescriptions are filled with drugs whose active ingredients are extracted or derived from plants. Worldwide sales of plant-based drugs are more than $40 billion each year.

Today, pharmaceutical companies analyze rain forest medications in laboratories. Because of scientific advances, many medications are produced today in laboratories using chemical compounds that mirror the chemical structure of the original plants in order to meet the world's growing demands. Some medications, however, still use the plant itself. A concern with conservationists is not to harvest plants from the wild to the point of threatening or endangering them, or causing their extinction. There is still a lot of work that needs to be done testing the medicinal value of plants. Currently, only 2% have been thoroughly studied for chemicals with potential medicinal use.

There are many well-established examples of medicinal plants. For example, the rosy periwinkle of Madagascar contains the alkaloids that can help cure people of Hodgkin's disease. The Madagascar periwinkle—now extinct in the wild due to deforestation of the Madagascar rain forest—has also increased the chances of survival for children with leukemia from 20% to 80%.

Atropine from a plant called belladonna is used in eye surgery. Atropine enlarges the eye's pupils. Ipecacuanha, which comes from a plant in Brazil, is used if someone accidentally swallows something poisonous. Ipecac syrup makes them vomit to get rid of the poison. Curare is used as a drug in general anesthesia. Ergot is used to treat severe migraine headaches. A substance from the saliva of the Central and South American vampire bat may be able to prevent heart attacks. The Pacific yew tree contains a compound called Taxol that fights cancer.

More than 25% of the active ingredients in today's cancer-fighting drugs come from organisms found only in the rain forest. The U.S. National Cancer Institute has identified more than 3,000 plants that are active against cancer cells, 70% of which are in the tropical forests. Researchers believe that many plants are waiting to be discovered that will provide treatments for constantly evolving pathogens such as bacteria, viruses, and fungi that are currently mutating against our mainstream drugs and becoming resistant to them. These pathogens cause serious diseases, including hepatitis, pneumonia, tuberculosis, and HIV, all of which are becoming difficult to treat. Experts believe that if there is a cure for diseases such as cancer or AIDS, it will be discovered in the rain forest.

Another branch of medicinal use is herbal medicine. Herbal medicine, or green medicine, refers to the use of any plant's seeds, berries, roots, leaves, bark, or flowers for medicinal purposes. In many countries, especially those where doctors or hospitals are not readily available, some medicines are still made directly from plants. About 80% of the people in the world rely on herbal medicines for some part of their primary health care.

Aromatherapy is another application of the soothing and healing benefits of forest plants.

Think of a time when you have walked into a favorite restaurant or a bakery. The aroma (smell) alone can make your mouth water in anticipation. If your grandmother or someone else you love is associated with the smell of roses, chances are each time you smell roses it will remind you of that person and create a warm, loving feeling.

This is how aromatherapy works. Aromatherapy is the use of plant oils that are believed to promote psychological and physical well being. The aroma of some natural plant oils stimulates the brain to trigger a reaction, and also provides physical benefits when it is inhaled directly into the lungs. Other oils that are applied to the skin can be absorbed into the bloodstream to provide the same benefits.

Aromatherapy can help with a physical condition, can help with symptoms, can affect one's mood, or can help relieve or temporarily eliminate stress and other psychological factors.

Although aromatherapy will not cure serious illnesses—such as cancer—it can help improve a cancer patient's quality of life by enhancing the patient's mood, calming fear, and easing nausea during chemotherapy treatments.

Aromatherapy is not intended to substitute for traditional medical care; it is meant to complement it. Many experts believe it can help with many common ailments such as cuts, bruises, acne, indigestion, PMS, hygiene, and inflammation. It can also provide mental and emotional assistance with stress, fatigue, fear, and anxiety.

It has other practical uses, as well. Some oils, for instance, act as a natural repellent and pesticide. One common product is the citronella candle that is used during the summer to keep mosquitoes away. Oils from lavender and peppermint are also a natural repellent against insects. Sprinkling a few drops of oil near a doorway or window will help repel insects.

BIOPROSPECTING

Bioprospecting is a fairly new endeavor of the scientific community to search, locate, and study the potential medicinal benefits of plants and animals from the rain forest and other ecosystems. In 1983, there were no U.S. pharmaceutical manufacturers involved in research programs to discover new drugs or cures from plants. Today, more than 100 pharmaceutical companies, as well as branches of the U.S. government—including the National Cancer Institute—are engaged in plant-based research projects that are trying to find possible drugs to treat infections, disorders, and serious life-threatening disease.

The majority of this research is currently taking place in the rain forest in an industry referred to as *bioprospecting*. In order to make all this work, it requires the combined expertise and efforts of many specialists, including plant collectors, botanists, biologists, anthropologists, ecologists and conservationists, natural product companies and nutritional supplement manufacturers, chemists, human disease researchers and health-care specialists, commercial drug companies, and native indigenous shamans. A major goal for bioprospectors is to preserve the rain forests by showing how much more valuable they are when kept intact.

In order for this to be realistic and successful, private industry, private landowners, and governments will have to learn to work together. Since the wealth and technology are concentrated in the developed countries, such as the United States, working relationships will need to be put in place so that it is fair and equitable to everyone involved in making bioprospecting a success. In addition, it is also critical to be methodical in this research, carefully planning each step with conservation in mind. If bioprospecting is done carefully, it can satisfy both economic and conservation goals while benefiting people with the discoveries in medical research and agricultural advances that combat disease and help supply food to growing populations.

THE VALUE OF URBAN FORESTS

Urban forests are planted communities of trees, shrubs, and grasses that exist in specially reserved areas within, and on the outskirts of, urban areas. Urban forest nontimber products are another important source of goods and services that forests offer. Foresters have long realized, and valued, the benefits provided by urban forests, such as improved air quality, cooling effects, wind control, soil stabilization, wildlife habitat, and scenic beauty and solitude.

Urban forests also produce goods such as chestnuts, mushrooms, raspberries, grapes, strawberries, peaches, mulberries, maple syrup, and honey. Horticultural (plants people grow in their yards) goods include walnuts, chestnuts, acorns, bamboo, ferns, oak seedlings, and native azaleas.

Medicinal products obtained from urban forests include sassafras bark, jewel weed, bee pollen, and maitake mushrooms. Craft resources include decorative greens, pinecones, pine boughs, boxwood, grapevine, forsythia sprigs, and willow bark. Recreational and aesthetic values include picnics, barbeques, hiking, nature walks, bird-watching, and in some areas, rock climbing.

Urban forest planning is a new field in urban land management and can help policymakers gain a better understanding for the potential importance of urban forest products, which will lead to better policies and management strategies that promote sustainable forest use.

TOURISM AND AESTHETIC VALUES

Through recreation and tourism, it is possible to use and enjoy forests without exploiting them. Forests attract people with all types of interests—fishing, hiking through the woods, camping next to a lake, mountain biking, going on a picnic, sitting at the base of a towering tree, rock climbing, kayaking, riding a horse through a meadow, bird-watching, wildlife viewing, and backpacking, to name a few. With the plentiful number of national forests in the United States (see Appendix), there are many places tourists can go to experience the fun, peace, and solitude of the forest environment. Each year, billions of dollars are spent in the tourism industry, and forests are popular places to visit.

According to the U.S. Forest Service, unlike logging an area (where once all the trees are cut down no more money comes into the area for at least 80 years—the time it takes for a new forest to grow), tourism is a healthy and environmentally friendly approach to the use of forests. When forests are left intact, visitors can visit year after year—and many tourists do just that.

Hiking in forests is a popular pastime for millions of tourists who visit the national forests in the United States each year. This area is the Wasatch-Cache National Forest in the Uinta Mountains of Utah. *(Photo courtesy Nature's Images)*

There are so many unique flowers in the rain forest that only 2% have been tested for their medicinal benefits. The majority of flowers and plants still need to be analyzed—scientists believe the cures to many serious diseases may exist in some of these untested flowers. *(Photo courtesy Nature's Images)*

Tourists also visit the rain forests in order to see what they are like and experience the wonders found within them. This is another reason for keeping rain forests intact.

With use of the land, however, comes the need for responsible action while visiting forests—for example, leaving trees and flowers intact; staying on the trails; packing out garbage; not bringing motorized OHVs into areas that are restricted; watching, but not interfering with, wildlife; and respecting others' rights to solitude. There are also aesthetic benefits from spending time in forests. Many people like to drive through, or hike in, the forested areas in the fall in order to see the changing colors of leaves. These are the benefits from forests that are hard to measure—intangible benefits.

MANAGEMENT OF FOREST RESOURCES IN A RAPIDLY CHANGING WORLD

Given good management, trees are a renewable natural resource that provide many useful products, including fuel, lumber, wood pulp, fiber, and food for human and animal consumption. Fundamental to creating a successful management program is the understanding that forests are recognized as a community of interacting plants, animals, soil, water, air, and people within a major landscape—they are no longer thought of as just a bunch of trees.

Forest management in the twenty-first century involves more than just harvesting trees for income. It requires that professional foresters (forest managers) recognize how forest management impacts forest health, wildlife, soils, and water quality; and how forestry can be used as a tool to improve and protect other natural resources.

Responsible forest management is based on ecological sustainability that conserves native species of plants and animals and their habitat. Rivers and streams must also be protected, and planning must focus on what needs to be done to support the ecosystem instead of only concentrating on removing huge volumes of timber, as was the general practice in the past for many forests.

This chapter looks at the components of a well-managed forest, the role of the U.S. Forest Service, high-tech computer tools that help forest managers make well-informed decisions, fire management, and the value of sustainable forestry. It then looks at applying the successful management techniques of developed countries' forests to those of the rain forests in developing countries. It also examines forest management for private forest landowners. Finally, it explores what everyone can do to promote and ensure the health of forests.

COMPONENTS OF A WELL-MANAGED FOREST

Because there is such a wide diversity of resources found within the boundaries of forests, the balancing act of managing them can be a challenge for forest managers (also called foresters). It is important to look at the "big picture" when developing workable management plans. Forest managers and other scientists must look at the big picture, because everything is related—every living and nonliving thing are connected in an ecosystem. Because the conditions of the natural world are always changing, effective forest managers must also monitor these changes and occasionally adjust their management plans to encompass the change. This is especially important in forests because much demand is put on the public lands for multiple uses.

There are several elements necessary in order to have a healthy, productive, well-managed forest. Ideally, a forest management plan should be put in place while a forest is young, and it must be based on the overall ecosystem. First, the biological diversity needs to be considered, not only for a small area, but also at the landscape level—such as an entire drainage basin. Looking at a larger scale is important for understanding the presence and roles of different plant and animal communities. Sometimes, if a forest is managed without the big picture in mind, it can contribute to some species becoming endangered or extinct. If species that are threatened can be identified, then the forest ecosystem can be managed to protect them. Also, the forest's diversity,

uniqueness, and risks (such as pests, fire, and weather) need to be identified and put into a management plan.

When looking at production—such as goods and products from
the forests—both timber and nontimber products need to be identified, along with the effect that removal of resources from the forest
would have on the natural ecosystem there. When managing forests for
timber production, foresters must look at the specific tree types and
understand their growth and mortality cycles to determine how often
a particular area will be able to be reforested. Once the trees are cut
down, their regeneration after harvest must be planned out so that the
ground is not left for invasive species to dominate, but for the forest to
regenerate with the species that the ecosystem previously supported.

Specialists dealing with wildlife habitat must also be involved in
the management planning so that the animal species are not negatively
impacted through disruption of the food chain or removal of critical
shelter. The overall health of the forest and its entire landscape (watershed) must be planned for. This includes selecting the right tree species,
thinning out appropriately aged trees, as well as addressing integrated
pest (insect) management.

Fuel loading—the amount of available dead timber for burning—
must be carefully monitored. Grazing must be managed to prevent
destruction of the natural grasses. Protecting soil and water resources
is also important. Soils in the forest are commonly mapped, so that
foresters can control and protect soil stability, water quality, and soil
productivity. Managers also try to consider the carbon cycle and manage the forests in a way that enhances it.

Socioeconomic benefits and impacts are also assessed. Specialists
not only consider the demand for wood products but also manage the
land for recreation and tourism. Unique biological, ecological, geologic,
and cultural sites are considered in a forest management plan. Once all
of these healthy management practices are decided on, the plan must
comply with the local, state, and federal laws that govern them.

Consideration of erosion and watershed management are also
important in forestry. Large-scale clear-cutting can cause erosion,

waterway and reservoir silting, damage to fisheries, and loss of drinkable or usable water. Modern methods of forest management also include the replanting of trees (called reforestation) and the planting of trees alongside crops (called agroforestry).

THE FUNCTIONS AND GOALS OF THE U.S. FOREST SERVICE

The goal of the U.S. Forest Service is to manage the national forests in an environmentally sound manner. Their top priority is to improve and maintain the health, diversity, and productivity of forest ecosystems for the enjoyment of current and future generations. The Forest Service's management strategies include guidance, administration, and support of the agency's forest products management and sales programs.

According to the U.S. Forest Service, the national forests were originally envisioned as working forests with multiple objectives: to improve and protect the forests, to create clean watershed systems, and to furnish a supply of timber for the citizens of the United States. Over time, forest management objectives have expanded and evolved to include ecological restoration and protection, research and product development, fire hazard reduction, and the maintenance of healthy forests.

Three periods in U.S. history have shaped the national forests into what they are today. The founders of the early national forests saw them as working forests with multiple objectives. The Organic Administration Act of 1897, under which most national forests were established, set forth the legal policy of protecting the forested lands and providing timber as a natural resource.

Several national forests were later created under the Weeks Law of 1911 in order to restore forests on formerly private land that had been heavily logged or cleared for agriculture. Many of today's eastern national forests were acquired under the Week's Law.

Until World War II, the Forest Service mainly focused on watershed protection, forest restoration, and wildfire prevention and suppression. Since there were abundant supplies of private timber, very little national forest logging occurred during this time period.

After World War II, a housing boom occurred, and Americans viewed the national forests as a convenient supply of building material. Clear-cutting for building lumber became a widespread practice; but along with the increased logging, many citizens became concerned about environmental issues and the possible destruction of the forests.

In the 1960s and 1970s, several laws were made to protect forests. Other laws helped develop the concept of "multiple use" management—where uses of timber, forage, and water shared equal importance with wildlife conservation and recreational opportunities. Today, logging is controlled to the point that America imports more wood each year from other countries than it exports.

Today, the Forest Service has multiple goals—environmental protection, research and product development, ecological restoration, hazard reduction, healthy forests, and planning for the future. Because of environmental concerns in the 1970s, the Forest Service has developed and practices some of the most effective environmental protection policies in the world. In response to the public controversy and a better understanding of how management actions influence the landscape, today's timber sale levels have dropped by two-thirds (back to the pre-1950 levels), even though timber demand continues to increase about 1% each year. In addition, clear-cut harvests have been decreased by 80% over the past 10 years.

The Forest Service conducts considerable research in the effort to find more effective ways of managing forests in an ecologically sound manner. The knowledge gained through research helps forest managers worldwide—not just in the United States.

A key area of research is in improving forest resource conservation. Research has helped reduce wood use and industrial pollution through the development of wood composites—such as fiberboard, improved pulping operations, and development in the use of recycled wood products. The multiple benefits that result from this research is shared freely with private industry and usually results in more environmentally efficient operations.

An important part of the Forest Service's management strategy is to reduce hazards. For example, consider areas where the ecosystems need to have frequent low-intensity fires, such as western ponderosa pine ecosystems. If these areas have not been allowed to frequently burn, they become vulnerable to high-intensity crown fires. In these areas, the Forest Service reduces the fire hazard by thinning out the overcrowded fire-intolerant tree species and manages the land so that it will support the natural low-intensity fire patterns that occur in healthy forests.

Forest Facts

- There are 155 national forests in the United States. The U.S. Forest Service manages forested lands in 44 states, Puerto Rico, and the U.S. Virgin Islands.
- National forests encompass 191 million acres of land—roughly the size of Texas.
- Two-thirds of forested lands (504 million acres) are timberland-forested areas that supply wood for loggers to harvest. About 52 million acres is reserved for nontimber uses, such as parks and wilderness areas.
- Of all the official designated forest wilderness lands in the United States, 56% are located in Alaska.
- There are 644 forest wilderness areas.
- There are 95 designated wild and scenic rivers.
- The national forests have 133,087 miles (214,173 km) of trails; 4,300 campgrounds; 135 alpine ski areas; 1,496 picnic sites; and 18,000 recreation facilities.
- Over the last 10 years, forest products companies have spent more than $100 million on wildlife and environmental research.
- Due to careful forest management, the white-tailed deer population has grown from 4.5 million to over 16 million in the past 30 years. Likewise, pronghorn antelope have gone from near extinction to more than one million today.

(Source: U.S. Forest Service)

The Forest Service also strives to maintain the ecological health of a forest area. For example, in the southern part of the United States, the Forest Service protects the environment for the red-cockaded wood-pecker (an endangered species) by developing site-specific management plans, which protects their habitat.

The Forest Service manages their forests at the landscape level—not just a tree level. Their goal is to be able to ensure the long-term health of the land. This is accomplished through restoration and maintenance of healthy forests.

The Forest Service is also planning for the future. Each individual forest develops a plan that allows public involvement and sound scientific practices to guide future management. Timber harvest issues, in particular, are extremely important to the future of America's federal forests.

MODELING, MANAGING, AND PLANNING

In order to manage forests—whether it is small parcels or large areas—it is important for the manager to understand the geographic area as well as all the components within the ecosystem and how they relate to, and depend on, each other. With the development of computers and sophisticated software over the past few years, modern technology has enabled scientists and managers to build mathematical and virtual models to represent forest landscapes and the systems that function on them. Computer modeling can help unravel the complex relationships so that forest managers can not only manage the land at the present time, but also project into the future and be able to create long-term management plans.

These computer models involve intricate mathematical equations and solutions; many involve complex mathematical algorithms and statistical analyses. Models can answer questions and provide guidance in such fields as forest development, logging management, engineering planning (such as for campground, rest stops, hiking trails, boat docks, and other recreational developments), inventory analysis, ecosystem analysis, forest health analysis, terrain stability determination, archaeological study, fishery plans, wildlife habitat, and recreational development and monitoring.

The Forest Service employs many scientific specialists. Geologists use models to locate potential mineral deposits; hydrologists are able to model flow and surface water quality, as well as watershed analysis; wildlife biologists can model wildlife habitat; and firefighters and ecologists can model wildfire patterns and the various effects from wind, terrain, and vegetation. In fact, modeling can be done for anything of interest to scientists and land managers. The more scientists learn, the more sophisticated the models become.

Scientists who build these models must have a detailed understanding of the terrain and the systems that affect them (such as the hydrologic cycle); the life-forms (plants and animals) within the system and their functions; the physical and geologic processes that occur (such as erosion, deposition, and the nitrogen cycle); weather patterns; and a host of other physical phenomenon.

The more data (data input) a model has, the better it is able to represent reality, and the more useful the model is. With models, cause-and-effect scenarios can be developed so that managers can analyze the possible short- and long-term effects and consequences of their decisions on the landscape. In this way, fewer mistakes are likely to be made that could harm the environment. Models help create better short- and long-term management plans.

GEOGRAPHIC ANALYSIS AND MAPPING—HIGH-TECH TOOLS TO HELP FOREST MANAGERS

Because of all the decisions that forest managers must make and all the issues they must take into consideration, their work can quickly become overwhelming. Fortunately, technology has advanced far enough that tools have been developed to handle large amounts of interactive data. A significant addition to the science of mathematical modeling is the use of the rapidly evolving technologies of Geographic Information Systems (GIS), remote sensing technology (using satellite imagery), and real-time monitoring.

A Geographic Information System—or GIS—involves a powerful, complex computer database that organizes information about a specific

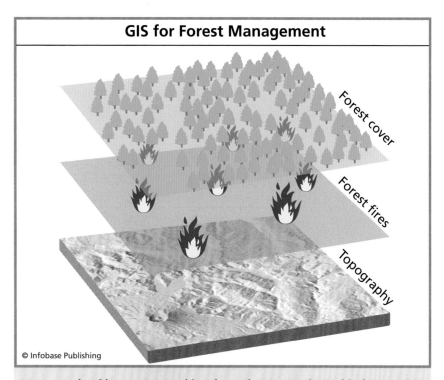

GIS for Forest Management

An example of how a Geographic Information System is used in forest management. This map allows forest managers to correlate forest fires with forest cover and topography.

location. It creates a computerized map with a potentially unlimited amount of information available for every place on the map. One advantage of GIS over paper maps is that many more layers can be stored and easily displayed in various combinations.

The real strength of GIS lies in its potential to assist scientists and forest managers in analyzing data and making informed decisions. Stacking themes or layers of information allows new patterns to emerge for scientific consideration. When information concerning different resources—such as wildlife, minerals, plants, hydrology (water), and soils—is entered into GIS, managers can look across disciplines and see the big picture. For example, endangered species habitats can be seen along with standard hydrology and vegetation maps.

GIS technology is used by forest resource managers for a number of purposes such as determining suitability of an area for wildlife habitat, mapping areas at risk for fire, or assessing the health of rangelands and riparian areas in order to manage the health of wildlife.

Another advantage of GIS is its ability to show changes over time. By comparing old data with new data for the same location, it is possible to see which areas have changed and have been impacted the most. Trends can also be projected into the future. GIS technology alone has changed the way natural resource decisions are made. Maps and products associated with these efforts assist not only the foresters but also planners, policy makers, and concerned citizens because they provide consistent information.

Another tool is remote sensing: the collection and measurement of information by a device not in physical contact with what it is observing. Common remote sensing devices include eyes, cameras, binoculars, microscopes, telescopes, video cameras, and satellites. Input from remote sensors—usually aerial photos taken from an airplane or images acquired from a satellite—provide important information to a GIS in order to help forest managers make decisions.

Remote sensing imaging systems can see better than the human eye—they can see in more wavelengths of light. This ability to see multispectral (multiple band) energy allows remote sensors to have greater capabilities than our eyes. Computer software—called image processing software—is used to analyze remotely sensed images because it can see those subtle differences that the human eye is unable to see; therefore, image processing software can supply meaningful information that no other analytical method can provide. This information can be put into a GIS in order to inventory a forest, model processes in the forest, identify areas where significant change has occurred, map off-highway-vehicle (OHV) damage, detect invasive weed species, measure forest biomass and amounts of timber, study trends of dwindling open space, monitor deforestation, map fuel buildup and fire dangers in the forest, map existing vegetation, and help forest managers make responsible short- and long-term decisions.

Another method forest managers use to model the landscape and make quick decisions is through real-time monitoring and reporting. This data can then be used in a GIS environment to solve specific forest resource issues.

Real-time data can be collected for forest wildfires, water resources, volcano hazards, landslide hazards, earthquake hazards, groundwater and surface water issues, precipitation monitoring, flood hazards, water quality issues, drought monitoring, and stream flow monitoring. Real-time data is generally used for rapidly evolving, time-sensitive environmental land issues.

Computers allow for the development of much more sophisticated and accurate data to be compiled into maps, which helps scientists and land managers understand the processes in the forests better. Spatial analysis and modeling can be done to create analytical and predictive mapping, predictive ecosystem mapping, and planning for the short and long term.

FIRE MANAGEMENT

Although forest fires may seem like a bad thing, that is not always the case. Aboriginal people worldwide have understood the importance of fire in ecosystems and have used it as a tool for centuries to manage their environment.

Forests—such as those in the United States—have a complex relationship with fire that is essential to their health. Fire puts nutrients back into the soil by breaking down plant matter and kills insects and other pathogens. It also clears areas for smaller plants to establish themselves and allows light to reach the forest floor, which helps increase the diversity of life within the forest. Fire is also important for creating small openings—or habitat patches—for wildlife such as deer, moose, elk, caribou, quail, and many others; these animals are most healthy when the forest has a high level of diversity.

Another benefit of periodic fire is that it lowers the density of forests, which then reduces competition for sunlight and water. When trees do not have to compete for these things, they are better able to fight disease and insect outbreaks.

In hard-to-reach areas, planes discharge a layer of fire retardant over the forest fires. Multiple passes are required to contain a fire. *(Courtesy U.S. Department of Agriculture)*

Forest managers have learned over the years that fire suppression—keeping areas from burning and putting out actual fires quickly—is actually bad for the health of a forest. When fires are put out quickly to "protect" timber and private property, it allows dead plant matter (dead trees, leaves, small shrubs, and brush) to collect on the forest floor, which creates larger and larger fuel loads. When this happens, instead of having small fires that occur frequently, the entire forest can catch fire and, with the fuel loads on the ground, create a fire that does much more damage and is much more difficult to put out.

Because small forest fires were prevented in the past, the fine balance of nature was upset. Old management policies led to the destruction of forests that would have survived in much better condition if small fires had been allowed to run their course. Under normal conditions, fires sweep through dry forests every five to twenty years. Because of this, the fuel loads are small and the fire only burns small shrubs and disease-ridden trees. Other trees with thick bark usually survive the fire.

Forests with high fuel loads can burn hotter and be more destructive than forests that have occasional fires sweeping through and clearing out the high fuel loads. *(Courtesy Bureau of Land Management, photo by Kelly Rigby)*

Forest managers have learned from the dangers of fire suppression and changed their policies accordingly. They have learned that by creating occasional fires, high fuel load buildups can be prevented so that if a wildfire does start in a forest (such as from a lightning strike), it will not be an intensive fire that burns hot and gets out of control.

Purposely created fires are called "controlled burns." They are usually started during a wetter season, so that there is not as great a chance of them getting out of control and becoming a hard-to-manage wildfire. Managers have determined that controlled burns are less expensive than thinning trees out of the forest. They also are ecologically more similar to natural disturbances, and therefore, more environmentally friendly. Another important component to preventing forest wildfires is to educate people on how to prevent human-caused fires.

SUSTAINABLE FORESTRY—LONG-TERM PROTECTION OF THE REMAINING FORESTS

In order to create sustainable forests—keeping a forest ecosystem healthy so that it can constantly renew and replenish itself at a consistent level—it is necessary to manage forest lands as a stewardship by having designated managers and others take responsibility and care

Important Fire Rules and Facts

- Make campfires only in designated areas.
- Never leave a campfire unattended.
- Always keep water near a campfire.
- Put out a campfire by following these simple steps:
  1. Drown the fire with water.
  2. Use a stick to mix the ashes with the soil.
  3. Scrape and chop partially burned sticks.
  4. Add more water.
  5. Stir the soil again.

(Source: U.S. Forest Service)

of the resources and their maintenance. According to the Rainforest Alliance, more than 6 billion people rely on trees and plants to build houses, make furniture, heat their homes, and produce products like paper, which makes the pressures on the world's forests enormous.

With the world population continuing to increase—it is projected to increase another 1.5 billion over the next 20 years—it is important for all living species that the Earth's forests are managed in a sustainable way. In order to achieve these goals, the adoption of sustainable management programs must be put in place today in order to plan for the future.

In general, forests in the developed countries are already managed in this way. Forests in the developing countries—many of which are rain forests—need to be managed in a similar way in order to keep these forests in existence for the long term. Many environmental organizations, both in the United States and other countries, are currently involved in efforts to assist developing countries in developing sustainable forest management plans.

One method of promoting this is through an incentive program where certification is provided on wood products originating from forests that are managed to conserve biodiversity and also support local communities. In this system, the businesses that practice conservation would get business over those that do not—thereby rewarding and encouraging responsible conservation.

For example, a program of woody biomass utilization, run by the U.S. Forest Service, also keys in on sustainability. Instead of clear-cutting new lumber, woody biomass is collected and used instead. Woody biomass is the material from trees and woody plants (including limbs, needles, tops, leaves, and other woody parts) that are grown in a forest. This material is the by-product of forest management, ecosystem restoration, or hazardous fuel reduction. This program harvests and makes available the use of woody biomass to produce a full range of wood products. These products include timber, engineered lumber, paper and pulp, and furniture; as well as bioenergy, biofuels (such as ethanol and diesel), and bio-based products (such as plastics and solvents).

In this way, the forest is utilized for many important goods and services, but less of the forest needs to be chopped down. This is an important step toward sustainable forestry.

There are several practices that can be used to ensure the future vitality of forests, such as through the establishment of protected area networks. When lands are set aside to function as forests, then other activities are excluded, such as urbanization, mining, or other invasive uses of the land. Foresters can also establish rates of sustainable timber harvesting. This is not to say that trees cannot be cut down for wood products, but instead only a certain amount in an area over time are cut. This ensures that the rate of cutting does not exceed that of replanting and growing. This keeps forests from being used up and disappearing.

Agroforestry is another way to make the land produce goods, while still maintaining a forest. This is the practice of utilizing the forest floor to grow crops. This way, food can be grown without negatively impacting forested areas by clearing the trees out; rather, the two land uses are done jointly.

Expanding tree plantations is another way for conserving forests. On tree plantations, trees are planted, cultivated, and harvested for many purposes, such as landscaping and providing products made from wood. In this way, humans are still able to obtain the products they need without impacting forests. It is also possible to restore degraded lands. Land that has been previously farmed, eroded, or overcut can be restored with careful management and converted back into forested areas.

According to the U.S. Forest Service, sometimes it is necessary to create new laws and regulations in the government policies that control the land. If practices are occurring that are threatening the future of the forest, they must be changed. For example, if the current forest policy allows more timber to be cut than is growing back, those cultivation limits must be lowered. If recreational activities, such as camping or riding OHVs, are causing erosion in the forest and threatening the health of the ecosystem, these practices need to be changed, and new guidelines and policies put in place.

Other important factors in creating and ensuring sustainable forestry are research, education, and public awareness. The more research scientists accomplish, the more they understand about the forest ecosystem, which then creates opportunities to improve forest health. For example, foresters used to believe all wildfires were bad. Through extensive research, they were better able to understand environmentally the role fire plays in the entire ecosystem. Education and awareness of the public is also important for the continuing health of the forests. Education about the enormous potential of the rain forests has made attempts at conservation possible. Many public schools in the United States get involved in rain forest conservation by allowing students and sponsors to "buy" (adopt) areas of rain forest that are guaranteed to be protected long term. When the public learns the value of natural resources in forests, they are more likely to participate in the conservation process.

APPLYING MANAGEMENT KNOWLEDGE TO THE RAIN FOREST

Protection and regeneration of the rain forests is a key goal of many environmental organizations. Various organizations—such as the World Wildlife Fund and the Rain Forest Alliance—attempt to educate people who may never have seen, or will see, a rain forest in person, about the marvelous resources these forests contain. By conducting international conferences to talk about conservation strategies, they are educating others so that informed conservation decisions can be made now and planned for the long-term future.

One method of encouraging sustainable forest management in the rain forests is by dividing the land and creating individual management units of about 267,000 acres (100,000 hectares) in size. These plots of land are awarded to inhabitants for a period of 99 years. In order to have the land, they must prepare land use plans that will ensure long-term sustainability of the natural forest resources. The land use plan must also take into account the wildlife in the area and provide for its health as well.

The same types of management practices that are used in temperate forests are also applicable to rain forests. For example, creating **reserves** where the forests are left intact and preserved—much like the designated wilderness areas in the United States—is one way to manage the rain forest. Involving the inhabitants of the forest in the role of stewardship is another option. By educating the people that live in the rain forest about the global impacts of rain forest deforestation, and involving them in the decision-making, they can have a bigger interest in the outcome.

Computer modeling is another tool that can be used to manage the rain forests by the gathering of data and the improvement of the knowledge base, which enables scientists, managers, and inhabitants to make better-informed decisions. For example, instead of selling land to loggers in order to get quick cash, inhabitants may be less tempted if they were more aware of the long-term consequences of forest destruction. Along these same lines, another possibility of protecting the forests is for governments to offer incentives to the inhabitants to convince them that better management practices are the best solution. Because many of these areas have high amounts of poverty, selling timber to logging companies is tempting. If governments were to step in and subsidize (financially compensate) landowners to keep the land protected, conservation would become much more attractive.

Adopting sustainable timber harvest laws are also important. Such measures could include operating under a management plan that coincides with national forest management, restricting logging to "production" forests only, improving access roads, preserving forested buffer zones along waterways, and taking steps to ensure regeneration of logged-over stands.

Promoting agroforestry is another management option. Planting crops and grazing livestock on the same parcel of land that supports forests can improve land use and productivity at the same time.

Restoration of previously deforested land is another management option. This includes tree planting and the protection of existing vegetation from fire, grazing, and land clearing. This is another case where incentives can be offered to the landowner. Replanting degraded areas provides many ecological benefits. It renews the watershed's ability to regulate groundwater, reduce soil erosion, produce useful commercial crops, and store carbon from the atmosphere. When replanting, however, it is important that noninvasive species be planted in order to protect the local plant and animal life.

Another viable management option in trying to address the world demand for high value hardwoods (such as mahogany), is to grow these species on tropical tree farms. The sale of these tropical hardwoods reduces the pressure on the world's rain forests while, at the same time, it protects the natural rain forest habitat elsewhere by reducing the need to cut down trees and spread deforestation. One establishment that does this is a company called Tropical American Tree Farms. They not only manage tree plantations in the rain forest specifically set aside as a source of wood, they also manage their rain forest areas by actively providing habitat for the indigenous species of plants and animals. Their careful management of the rain forest land is an example of how rain forests everywhere can be managed in a sustainable way, long-term.

FOREST MANAGEMENT FOR PRIVATE FOREST LANDOWNERS

Some forest areas are owned by private landowners. Care of privately owned forests is just as important as the care of forests owned by states and federal government agencies. The same environmental impacts apply to all forested land, regardless of who owns them. In order to help private owners, many state and federal government agencies hold workshops and offer educational programs to teach landowners about sustainable forestry. They offer instruction on protecting soil resources and water quality. They also offer helpful information about the practice of agroforestry, wildlife habitat, and enhancement.

One program developed by the U.S. Forest Service is the Forest Legacy Program (FLP). The FLP was established in the 1990 Farm Bill to protect environmentally important forest areas that are threatened by conversion to nonforest uses. This program is geared toward sustainable forestry and resource protection for future generations. Its goal is to protect important fish and wildlife habitat, conserve watershed functions, and maintain recreational opportunities.

Since the FLP was begun in 1992, it has helped conserve more than 587,608 acres (237,797 hectares) in the United States—land valued at $250 million. Effective forest management for private landowners is accomplished using the same methods as other forests. Management begins with the creation of a Forest Management Plan. The plan should provide a report that outlines the short- and long-term management goals. Plans often include information on timber types, roads, rivers, lakes, streams, short- and long-term wildlife management objectives, soil information and analysis, and how the forest fits in with the larger landscape ecosystem.

According to Potlach Corporation of Forest Management, if a private forest is going to be logged, planning the logging operation is crucial in improving the value of the forest. Trees need to be identified that are important to preserve for wildlife habitat, those trees that can be harvested, and those trees that may face diseases. It must be decided how many trees can be removed without making the forest become unsustainable.

It is also important to manage and provide habitat for wildlife species, as well as devise a reforestation plan that will determine how many new trees will be planted, where, and what type of species are needed in order to maintain the health of the land while taking care to keep invasive species out.

DOING YOUR PART

There are things that everyone can do to help care for the forests. The U.S. Forest Service and the Bureau of Land Management suggest that you should do the following when visiting a forest:

- Plan ahead and prepare. Know the rules and learn about the area you will be visiting.
- Travel and camp on hard surfaces. Using hard surfaces prevents damage to soil and plants. Hard surfaces are

established trails and campsites, rock, gravel, dry grasses, and snow.

- Dispose of waste properly. Use trash cans for your garbage. If you are visiting an area where there are no trashcans, then take all trash away with you, including leftover food, litter, and toilet paper, in a sealed plastic bag. Human waste should be buried in a small hole 6–8 inches (15–20 cm) deep and at least 200 feet (60 m) from water, camp, and trails.
- Leave what you find. Leave rocks, plants, arrowheads, and other objects so that others can enjoy them. Do not build structures or dig trenches.
- Be careful with fire. Use a lightweight stove for cooking and use a candle lantern for light. Where fires are allowed, use fire rings that are already there and keep fires small. Only use sticks from the ground that can be broken by hand. Be sure to burn all wood and coals to ash, put out campfires completely, and then scatter the cool ashes.
- Respect wildlife. Watch wildlife from a distance and do not follow or approach animals. Never feed animals. Control pets at all times, or better yet, leave them at home.
- Be considerate of others. Respect other visitors and remember that they want to enjoy the outdoors, too. Take breaks and make camps away from trails and other visitors. Let nature's sounds—not radios or music players—be the ones that are heard. Avoid loud voices and noises.

When managers and users of the forest follow the same guidelines and ethics, it makes managing forests both a short- and long-term success for everyone.

CHAPTER 8

CONSERVATION OF FORESTS

A s illustrated in the last chapter, when forests are managed properly and kept healthy, they provide habitat for wildlife and plants. Healthy forests have healthy streams that are home to fish and other aquatic life. They also provide people with a chance to enjoy nature.

A healthy forest has many different species of trees growing in it, both young and old. A good mixture of trees and other plants means a variety of animals will be able to live in the forest. The food, water, and shelter that animals need to survive can all be found in a forest, if the forest is healthy. From years of experience, foresters have learned how to keep forests healthy. Forest managers must work hard to protect wildlife habitat. In order to keep a forest sustainable over time, practices must be put in place to conserve the natural resources in the forest. If forests are not conserved—which is only possible through well-thought-out management plans—then the forest ecosystem will not remain healthy, and the species in them may become endangered or extinct.

This chapter examines the reasons why forest conservation is important, the current threats to conservation, practical methods of successful conservation, protecting threatened and endangered species, worldwide conservation campaigns, and things everyone can do to help conserve forest resources.

WHY DO FORESTS NEED CONSERVATION?

Since forests have existed on Earth, many species of plants have been unable to adapt to changing conditions. Thousands of species, over time, have become extinct naturally. The natural extinction rate, however, is not as fast as the evolution of new species. When nature interferes (earthquake, flood, or volcanic eruptions), the balance is generally restored over time. Unfortunately, the same is not true for human influence. Humans continually upset the balance of any ecosystem they enter and reduce the ecosystem's natural diversity—and forests are no exception. The process of protecting species so that they will continue to exist now and in the future is called conservation.

In addition to government organizations, many private organizations have been created to promote this conservation of natural resources—both plant and animal. Plants are conserved in different ways depending on where they are located, how long they live, and the specific threats they face. The best form of conservation is to protect the plant in its natural habitat. In cases where the habitat is destroyed, however, the plant can be removed to a controlled garden. Sometimes plants can be protected inside a nature reserve in the wild. Seeds from very rare plants are sometimes stored and collected in seed banks. This keeps them from becoming extinct.

The basic concept of conservation is "use it, but do not use it up." If forests are used wisely they will always supply clean water, wood products, wildlife, outdoor recreation opportunities, and beauty. Forests are one of the Earth's most renewable resources—if managed with conservation in mind.

A first step in forest conservation is to protect the forest from insect and disease epidemics, wildfires, careless road building, poor logging practices, and livestock use. Wildfires can damage trees, burn seedlings, destroy property, and threaten lives. Controlled burns, however, as illustrated previously, are a useful tool in timber and wildlife management.

Insect and disease outbreaks are best prevented, or managed, by cultivating healthy, strong trees. Therefore, it is helpful to thin out weak, or crowded, trees. Careless road building and logging can damage the forest by compacting the soil and causing erosion.

Although all forests need to have their resources conserved, fortunately, many of the boreal forests of the world have not been subjected to the degradation that temperate and tropical forests have. This is because their climate is so harsh people do not want to live there.

Many temperate forests, especially in the eastern United States, were deforested in the 1800s. Through the introduction of conservation practices, as well as educating the public, these forests have been largely restored. Many of the forests in the western United States have remained intact because they are protected in national and state parks and reserves. Within these forests, if logging is permitted, conservationists promote selective cutting rather than clear-cutting, because clear-cutting removes all the trees in a plot and can encourage erosion. Selectively cutting leaves some trees and takes more time and effort, but it is usually better for the wildlife and the stability of the soil.

As we have seen throughout this book, conservation in the rain forest is important in order to protect the biological diversity and ecological functions. As discussed previously, rain forests are critical to conserve because of the important contributions they make toward the carbon cycle and biological diversity and richness. Through conservation, the valuable natural habitat can be managed on a sustainable basis. According to the World Wildlife Fund, scientists believe that every 30 seconds another 35 acres (13 hectares) of rain forest will disappear. Unfortunately, this means that within mere minutes, humans undo what natural evolution and adaptation took thousands of years to create. In some rain forest areas—such as Malaysia—certain forest

Many forests are protected in reserves. This boreal forest is the Yukon Flats National Wildlife Refuge in Alaska. *(Courtesy U.S. Fish and Wildlife Service, photo by Ted Heuer)*

types are only found in protected parks and wildlife reserves. If these areas were not conserved, some forest types would already be extinct.

THREATS TO CONSERVATION

There are many serious threats to the health and future of the Earth's forested lands, such as acid rain, pollution, logging, global climate change, urban development, water pollution, poaching, introduced invasive species, mining, recreational activities, and insect infestation. Humans cause or contribute to most of these threats, which makes it critical that forests be well-managed and their resources conserved in order to be sustained over time.

One of the most devastating human-caused impacts to forests is acid rain. All rain contains minimal amounts of harmless acids because it dissolves natural carbon dioxide and sulfur dioxide in the air. The problem arises, however, when human activities become involved. Cities pollute the air with gases from power stations, factories, cars, and homes when fuel is burned, putting large amounts of sulfur and nitrogen into the air. These chemicals then react with damp air to produce strong sulfuric and nitric acids. They can be carried for long distances in the atmosphere and fall as acid rain, which kills trees and other plants.

Acid rain and pollution can have far-reaching effects on forested landscapes. Scientists have found that air pollution weakens the health of trees, which makes them more likely to die from insects, cold, disease, and other natural factors.

Clear-cutting of forests continues on private lands and in national forests in the United States. The lumber is used to build houses and make other products. A major threat to the forest ecosystem is that besides losing trees, the trees replanted on forestland are of only a few selected species. Therefore, the forest becomes more like a farm than an actual forest with many interconnected animal and plant species. This lowers the diversity of the immediate ecosystem—instead of supporting multiple species, it supports only one.

Global climate change is another threat to forests. As greenhouse gases high up in the atmosphere continue to increase due to peoples' activities—cattle ranching, industrial plants, cars, and burning of tropical forests—the increased temperatures can affect the health of forests. Scientists have determined that increased carbon dioxide affects plant growth.

Urban development for living and recreation also has an impact on forests. Any type of development—homes, shopping malls, schools, parks, amusement parks, ski resorts, mountain retreats, roads, and industry—impacts the land, including forests. Often the forestland is permanently destroyed.

Because streams and lakes are important in the forest environment, the health of forest plants and animals depends on having clean sources of water. Today, many activities contribute toward polluting water resources, such as industrial chemical waste, runoff of pesticides and fertilizers from lawns, farms, logging, and other developments. When areas are cleared of trees and soil erosion is increased, sediments can flow into, and clog, rivers with silt and other sediments, thereby polluting the water. Increased silt to the water can kill fish.

Poaching is another problem faced in forests today. Despite the Endangered Species Act of 1973 and other laws protecting forest plants and wildlife, the illegal trade in rare plant and animal species continues to be a threat, such as with bears, wolves, and rare wildflowers. This problem does not only exist in the boreal and temperate forests; it is also a major problem in the rain forests. Many people kill rare animals and steal rare plants. Unfortunately, poaching exists in the fur trade, as jaguars and other animals are illegally hunted. Poaching parrots and lizards is another widespread problem. Parrots should never be purchased without a small metal band around their leg certifying they were acquired legally.

Introduced species—both plants and animals—are another threat to the future of forests. These invasive species compete with the natural species in forests and often cause their destruction, which further impacts the ecosystem and the food webs associated with it.

Mining activities in all types of forests can have a largely negative impact. Mining for coal, granite, and other resources involves stripping

Domestic parrots must be purchased with a metal leg band, certifying they were obtained legally and not poached from the rain forests of South America. This blue and gold macaw, named Trooper, has a band on her right leg. She was born in captivity in the United States. *(Photo courtesy Nature's Images)*

away forested lands to get to the rock underneath. Many acres of land become damaged to the extent that forests can not regrow on nutrient-depleted soils.

Off-highway vehicles (OHVs) are also a problem, especially in forests of the United States. Off-road vehicles—such as motorbikes and four-wheel vehicles—are especially destructive to forest ecosystems when their riders take them off designated trails. These vehicles tear up fragile plants, crush animal burrows, cause increased erosion, and scare wildlife in the area. They also ruin the solitude that many forest visitors come to enjoy. Unfortunately, in U.S. forests, when this type of environmental damage occurs, designated trails are permanently closed to all OHV activity, which also punishes those that do stay on the designated trails. In drier environments, damage such as this can take the forest more than a hundred years to recover from.

As more forests are destroyed to produce products such as paper, there are many associated environmental impacts that people need to be aware of—a situation that reinforces the need to be environmentally responsible and reduce, reuse, and recycle. For example, the recycling of paper is extremely helpful to not only the forests themselves but to the entire environment.

Producing paper is also energy intensive, using a significant amount of power, which also adds to pollution and resource degradation (from oil drilling, oil spills, coal mining, pipelines, and the construction of transmission lines). Worldwide, huge tracts of forest are being cut each year for paper pulp production. When old-growth forests are cut, it damages ecosystems that took thousands, even millions, of years to develop.

KEY CONSERVATION ISSUES

The key to effective forest conservation is in creating a sustainable environment. If interaction and use of the forest is done with the goal of renewability in mind, then forest resources will be conserved. According to the Natural Resources Conservation Service, forest degradation can be controlled through the implementation of sustainable timber harvesting and wise forest use. Wise measures include operating under a well-thought-out management plan, restricting logging to "production" forests (forests grown specifically for harvesting), improving access road construction and maintenance, preserving forested buffer zones along watercourses, minimizing damage from falling trees, and taking steps to ensure adequate regeneration of stands that have had the majority of their trees cut down.

Fortunately, in the past five years, more than 100 countries, comprising about 90% of the Earth's forested area and trade in forest

A Christmas tree farm in Iowa. This practice helps conserve trees in natural forested areas. *(Courtesy Natural Resources Conservation Service)*

products, have become involved in developing criteria for sustainable forest management. There has also been growing interest in timber certification as a means of encouraging producers to meet established environmental standards for timber harvesting. One program—called SmartWood (introduced by the Rainforest Alliance)—is a certification program that notifies consumers that the wood products they purchase come from forests that are managed to conserve biodiversity and support local communities.

Promoting the use of agroforestry is another useful conservation measure. Agroforestry is the practice of growing trees with agricultural crops or livestock on the same parcel of land. It has proved to be an effective tool for improving land use and for increased overall agricultural productivity. Agroforestry also helps agricultural production in many areas because the trees help control soil erosion, enhance soil fertility, and provide a productive microclimate for crops and livestock.

Another method to support conservation is through the use of tree plantations. Industrial plantations of fast-growing trees have a great potential for meeting market demand for forest products, while maintaining the natural forest ecosystems. For example, some tree farms in the United States are used to grow commercial Christmas trees. The ecology of a tree farm, however, is different from that of a natural forest. When only a few species are grown, cultivated, harvested, and the area replanted to begin the cycle again, the complex interwoven ecosystems present in a natural forest do not exist. Tree farms take the pressure for development off natural forests, which allows them to maintain their biodiversity.

Brazil and Zimbabwe are two countries that have illustrated how successful tree plantations can be when they are operated in an environmentally sustainable manner and profitably grow the raw materials for a thriving local forest products industry. If tree farms are established on degraded forest land or nonforest land, plantations can improve land use productivity. Scientists have estimated that all of the world's demand for pulpwood (to make paper) could be met by plantations that would occupy only 3% of the world's forest area. This would allow natural forests to be managed for environmental purposes instead of productivity.

Restoring degraded lands is another key conservation issue. Scientists estimate there are nearly 534 million acres (200 million hectares) of degraded land in tropical countries. Much of the degradation is the result of past deforestation. Tree planting and the protection of existing vegetation from fire, grazing, and land clearing are key ways to restore land. Replanting forests with multiple-use species also helps to renew a watershed's ability to regulate groundwater, reduce soil erosion, produce useful crops, and store carbon from the atmosphere.

According to the Center for International Forest Research, investing in more research also promotes conservation. Forestry research must happen at an international level in order to combat deforestation, because deforestation is a global issue. Government policies must be examined to ensure that laws and practices are set in place to promote conservation.

As people become more mobile and tourism increases, these activities must also be managed with conservation in mind in order to ensure sustainable forests. With millions of people traveling each year, tourism is a growing source of revenue for people living in areas that are rich in plant and animal life, and threatened with destruction. While tourism can lead to problems such as waste, habitat destruction, and the displacement of local people and wildlife, it also has the potential to provide incentives for education and conservation.

According to the Rainforest Alliance, sustainable tourism is one method countries are looking at to reduce negative impacts on the environment. This type of management includes the development of guidelines for sustainable tourism, providing training and information to forest inhabitants on environmentally sound management. The end result is a healthy balance between tourism and nature.

Another way to encourage conservation within rain forest villages is to provide community incentives to businesses that protect the natural resources in the area. In exchange for promoting sustainable forestry, they receive economic opportunities in the form of money grants. These community projects also help protect natural resources from illegal activities and forest fires. This way, the local inhabitants strive to use the forest in a sustainable manner, because it is in their best economic interests to do so.

Logging is one of the biggest conservation issues—especially in the rain forests. Experts say that the world's rain forests are currently disappearing at a rate of 6,000 acres every hour—the equivalent of about 4,000 football fields. Clear-cutting in forests causes rapid deforestation. Bare ground is left that will not be reforested at the same level again for decades. Many conservationists believe that instead of clear-cutting, trees should only be thinned (taking some trees out, but leaving the majority alone) and new trees should be planted when the older ones are cut down.

Because of the world's continual demand for wood, one solution is to harvest the wood from tree farms. Similar to the tree farms in the United States for the cultivation of Christmas trees, tropical tree farms—or plantations—are also used to cultivate and harvest exotic tropical hardwoods like mahogany and teak. Tree plantations help reduce the pressure on the world's natural rain forests by protecting natural areas from being destroyed. Some tropical tree plantations also serve as miniature wildlife preserves by providing wildlife habitat for plant and animal species indigenous to the area, protecting their immediate habitat from being logged. Some of these plantations also plant buffers of trees around the farms that will never be harvested. This provides new, permanent corridors of natural habitat connecting the patches, or islands, of remaining forest to allow the animals to move freely among the forested areas and extend their breeding and feeding ranges. Otherwise, if they remain isolated, their species may dwindle.

Trees are also planted along rivers and stream banks to protect and preserve waterways; on steep slopes to prevent erosion. Flowering, fruiting, and shelter trees are planted to attract and feed the local birds and animals, which include such rain forest wildlife as scarlet macaws, howler monkeys, Congo monkeys, capuchin monkeys, spider monkeys, squirrel monkeys, ocelots, jaguars, pumas (mountain lions or cougars), peccaries, and three-toed sloths. Many of these species are currently threatened or endangered, but the positive side is that through designated protected areas, they are beginning to make a comeback.

ENDANGERED PLANTS AND WHAT THAT MEANS

Because many natural habitats are being destroyed to make room for human activity, such as planting crops, building towns, developing industry, and constructing roads, many plants are becoming endangered. Scientists warn that each minute, 100 acres of natural forest are destroyed—and only 10 acres are replanted. Species of plants are becoming lost and damage from erosion is increasing because plants are being removed and bare soil is left behind. When it rains, the water does not get absorbed into the ground—it runs off, washes away soil, and causes flooding.

Climatologists are also concerned about the rapid removal of plants from the tropical rain forests. They believe it will adversely affect Earth's climate. The rain forest plants release huge amounts of water into the atmosphere and absorb most of the sun's energy falling on them.

As plants are impacted, they can become threatened, endangered— even extinct. Currently, only a small number of plants have been studied to determine their usefulness to humans. But if they become endangered, humans may never know what benefits they may have had.

DISAPPEARING SPECIES—PLANTS IN TROUBLE

In the United States, there are many species of plants that are found nowhere else in the world—such as the silversword of Hawaii, which only grows in the Haleakala volcano crater. More than 20,000 different species of plants are considered native to this country, but environmental scientists have determined that many of those plants may be in danger of disappearing.

One-fifth of the native plants in this country are labeled "rare." In order to be considered rare, a plant must meet one or more of the three following conditions: (1) a small population size, (2) a small geographic range, or (3) a small habitat. Plants can be rare for a variety of different reasons. Their habitats could be naturally rare, such as areas affected uniquely by geography or climate. They could also be unnaturally rare due to human influences such as (1) development, (2) pollution, (3) invasion by exotic species, (4) land degradation, or (5) overcollecting.

A species is considered endangered when it is in danger of becoming extinct in the near future if not protected. *Threatened* is a term used to describe species that are likely to become endangered soon, if they are not protected.

Rare native plants have an intangible benefit. Because they have evolved over millions of years, they have adapted to their own niches within ecosystems.

Many plants are trampled and destroyed by hikers intentionally or accidentally. To combat this problem, the U.S. Bureau of Land Management (BLM) promotes a policy called "Leave No Trace." This policy urges hikers to always hike on designated trails so that plants do not get broken or ruined. When in a natural setting, visitors should always make sure that they leave the area untouched and looking like they had never been there.

Collecting plants from the wild to plant in private yards is also harmful. Laws have been established to keep this from happening, but it is an increasing problem. Collecting pressures threaten such plants as cactuses, pitcher plants, and orchids because of their unique ornamental value.

Alien and exotic species can also have devastating effects on biodiversity as they out-compete or destroy native species. Some alien plants are intentionally introduced into the environment; some are unknowingly or accidentally introduced—but the negative effect is still the same.

About 4,000 plants native to the United States are of concern to conservationists and land managers. The green pitcher plant (*Sarracenia oreophila*) is a federally protected endangered plant that only exists in a few wild populations in Alabama and Georgia. Its limited range and specialized habitat make it the rarest of all pitcher plants. Because they are meat-eating plants, poachers (thieves) often steal them from the wild.

THE ENDANGERED SPECIES ACT

Many species, both known and unknown to science, are being lost forever. Even the lowest estimates put this loss at three species per day. Over the Earth's history, scientists believe a rate of one species becoming extinct per year is considered normal. If the human population doubles over the next 50 years, even greater pressure will be placed on the environment. In order to control the trend of human-induced extinctions of species, laws have to be put in place to protect species—both plant and animal.

The first step toward conservation is education, so that people understand why there is a threat and what will happen if present destruction is not stopped. The U.S. Fish and Wildlife Service—part of the federal government—uses information from biologists nationwide to decide which species are threatened and endangered throughout the country. Identified species can then become legally protected under the U.S. Endangered Species Act of 1973. Under this law, all plant species that are placed on the list of Endangered and Threatened Wildlife and Plants cannot be exported or imported, sold without permits, or removed from federal lands. The penalty is stiff: violators can be fined $100,000 and spend a year in jail.

Individual state governments also have measures in place to protect plants, usually through the state's department of conservation of natural resources. Many private organizations promote conservation as well. Several organizations operate botanical gardens (arboretums) that store and grow threatened and endangered species, in order to prevent extinction or be used for ecological restoration, research, and education/public awareness.

The first species chosen to be saved are those that conservationists believe to be in most immediate danger. They look at several issues to determine which species those are, such as type and extent of the threat, the cause of rarity, economic potential, geographic range, and the number of existing plants of that species. The biology of the plant, such as its reproduction, growth rate, and life span, are also considered.

High-priority species often include endemics (plants that are native to one specific area and exist nowhere else on Earth) because these species are very susceptible to environmental change and are often indicators of unique and rare habitats. For example, about 90% of Hawaii's

There are many endangered species in temperate and boreal forests, such as the gray wolf shown in the photo. It is important to understand that *endangered* means there is still time to save the species, but it takes a well-thought-out, dedicated recovery plan to do so. *(Photo courtesy of the U.S. Fish and Wildlife Service, photo by Gary Kramer)*

rain forest plants are endemic. They also have the highest percentage of endangered plants in the United States.

The initial concept for the Endangered Species Act was begun in 1966 with the establishment of the Endangered Species Preservation

Act. Unfortunately, it only listed rare and disappearing species but gave them no protection. The first effort to actually stop the loss of endangered species came with the enactment of the 1969 Endangered Species Conservation Act, which banned the import of species threatened with worldwide extinction.

Then, in 1973, President Richard M. Nixon signed into law the Endangered Species Act. This law focused on protecting species faced with imminent extinction. It focused on making the extinction of any species illegal. It banned the harming of listed species in any way, including the destruction of their habitat.

The act is one of the most far-reaching laws ever enacted by any country. Congress established this act because it recognized that all species "are of aesthetic, ecological, educational, historical, recreational, and scientific value to the Nation and its people." (Endangered Species Act, 1973).

Endangered species now receive considerable protection from the government. When a species is listed, the government has the opportunity to identify critical habitat for the species. After more than 30 years of having the Endangered Species Act in place, the result has been extremely effective. By focusing on protection of the species themselves, as well as conservation of the ecosystems on which they depend, our knowledge of ecological systems has expanded and our understanding of protecting and providing for species has greatly increased.

THE TESS LIST

The TESS list (Threatened and Endangered Species System list) is the official listing maintained by the U.S. Fish and Wildlife Service that identifies species that are threatened or endangered. The list is used to keep track of data, such as the historic range of the plant or animal, and how many individual plants or animals existed in the population at the time it was listed.

The listing of threatened and endangered species must follow specific guidelines. In order to request that a species be listed, a petition must be entered. Nominating officials check the species against a database of North American species and review the information over a 12-month period. If listing the species is warranted, the scientific community, the public, and federal and state government agencies then review it for two months. Once a species passes this level of review, it is officially added to the list of species in the *Federal Register*.

SMOKEY BEAR SAYS "ONLY YOU CAN PREVENT FOREST FIRES"

When the weather is hot, dry, or windy, or when thunderstorms occur, there is the danger of forest fire. The United States Forest Service has developed a system to calculate and distribute fire danger information and provide daily weather reports from more than 1,000 fire danger weather stations throughout the country.

Firefighters have expanded the tools they use to reduce and prevent forest fires that occur under these dangerous conditions. By setting

The Story of Smokey Bear

Smokey Bear is based on a real baby black bear that was found harmed, but alive, after a devastating wildfire in the Capitan Mountains of New Mexico. By the time the fire fighters arrived, the wind had spread the fire until it became a raging blaze. Many fire fighters pitched in to help—from the Forest Service, U.S. Army, and from the State Game Department. Even with all these fire fighters present, it was a huge task to get the fire under control because the wind spread it quickly from one place to another.

Then, in the midst of the hot fire zone, a bear cub showed up, alone—his mother apparently killed by the fire. When the flames surrounded the bear cub, he climbed a nearby tree to escape them. By the time the fire fighters rescued him, the forest was completely burned. The firefighters named him Smokey. This little cub is what inspired the Smokey Bear campaign: "Only YOU Can Prevent Forest Fires!" And the rest is history.

(Source: U.S. Forest Service)

controlled burns (small, monitored, intentionally set fires) the U.S. Forest Service clears forests of dry, dead debris. Controlled burns not only reduce dangerous undergrowth (also called "fire fuel"), but actually help many plants reproduce and increase food for wild animals. The largest benefit of controlled burns is that they lessen the possibility of an unplanned wildfire (caused by lightning or human carelessness) raging out of control.

There are thousands of brave men and women who fight forest fires. They can use water or they can remove the fuel from the fire by cutting down trees or setting small fires to create a firebreak. Firefighter's tools are limited because they have to carry them in to fight wildfires that are difficult to reach and combat. Therefore, it is important that every visitor to the forest practice forest safety.

Forest fires in the national forests of the United States can present problems for wildlife and people. In order to help conserve forest resources—especially from fires caused by peoples' careless behavior—the U.S. Forest Service began one of the most successful public service campaigns in U.S. history. Created in 1944, the Smokey Bear campaign is the longest running program of its type in history. Smokey Bear is one of the world's most recognizable fictional characters, earning him a unique place in America's culture.

HELPING THE FORESTS—CONSERVATION CAMPAIGNS

Even though rain forest conservation has been in the news frequently this past decade, they are still being destroyed at an alarming rate. As illustrated previously, conservation of boreal and temperate forests has been much more successful, for these forests are largely located in developed nations that have already put conservation plans in place. One program of the federal government for federal lands is the "Leave No Trace" concept.

The "Leave No Trace" program, adopted by the federal government and private organizations, is designed to educate outdoor recreation enthusiasts and build awareness of the environment and land stewardship. Its goal is to avoid, or minimize, impacts to natural area resources and help create a positive recreational experience for all visitors. This program is important because America's public lands are a finite resource whose social and ecological values are linked to the health of the land. Today, forest managers face a constant struggle in their efforts to find an appropriate balance between programs designed to preserve the land's natural and cultural resources and provide high-quality recreational use.

The Leave No Trace educational program is designed to teach visitors low-impact care of the environment. If visitors follow the program's guidelines and act responsibly when using the land, then more direct regulations will not be necessary, such as restricting the number of people that can visit a particular area at a time or having to police the public lands. The Leave No Trace program stresses the following actions in order to maintain the beauty of the land:

LEAVE NO TRACE!

Before You Go:
1. Obtain information about the area and use restrictions.
2. Plan your trip for "off season" or nonholiday times. If this is not possible, go to less popular areas.
3. Choose equipment in earth tone colors: blue, green, tan, etc.
4. Repackage food in lightweight, burnable, or packout containers.

On Your Way:
1. Stay on designated trails.
2. Do not cut across switchbacks.
3. When traveling cross-country, hike in small groups and spread out.
4. Do not get off muddy trails.
5. Avoid hanging signs and ribbons or carving on trees to mark travel routes.
6. When meeting horseback riders, step off lower side of trail, stand still, and talk quietly.

While You Are There:

Campsite:
1. If in high-use areas, choose existing campsites.
2. In remote areas, choose sites that cannot be damaged by your stay.
3. All campsites should be at least 75 paces from water and trails (200 feet).
4. Hide camp from view.
5. Do not dig trenches around tents.
6. Avoid building camp structures. If temporary structures are built, dismantle completely before leaving.

Campfires:
1. For cooking, use lightweight gas stove rather than a fire.
2. In areas where fires are permitted, use existing fire rings.
3. Do not build new fire rings.
4. Do not build fires against large rocks.
5. Learn and practice alternative fire building methods which Leave No Trace!
6. Use dead and down wood, no larger than the size of your forearm.
7. Do not break branches off trees.
8. Put fire completely out before leaving (cold to the touch).

Sanitation:
1. Deposit human waste and toilet paper in catholes. Catholes are 6 to 8 inches (15 to 20 cm) deep and should be located at least 75 paces from water or camp. Cover and disguise catholes when finished.
2. Wash dishes, clothes, and yourself away from natural water.
3. Cover latrine and wash water holes thoroughly before breaking camp.
4. Pick up all trash and pack it out (yours and others).

Courtesy:

1. Avoid loud music and voices or other loud noises.
2. Keep pets under control at all times. Better still, leave them home.
3. Leave flowers, artifacts, and picturesque rocks and snags for others to enjoy.

Before You Leave:

Take one last look at where you have been and do your best to—Leave No Trace!

(Leave No Trace text courtesy of the U.S. Bureau of Land Management)

Many individuals and environmental organizations are trying to find effective ways to conserve the Earth's tropical rain forests and the plants and animals that exist in them. Conservation organizations have employed several different conservation methods, such as establishing preserves (areas that are permanently protected against disturbance), encouraging the use of renewable resources that can be harvested (such as fruits and nuts), and working with governments to protect the rights of the people that live in the rain forest. Conservation organizations also work hard at educating not only those people that live in the rain forest about the valuable ecosystem and the treasures it contains, but also educating people that live in developed countries (such as in the United States) on how to use fewer resources. They educate people on the benefits to the environment of conserving, reducing, reusing, and recycling items (such as paper products) so that additional trees do not need to be cut down. Education also includes promoting the use of products that come only from properly managed forests—such as those that grow valuable hardwoods like mahogany—instead of harvesting trees from the natural rain forest ecosystem. Many conservation achievements come from making people aware of the short- and long-term effects of destroying the rain forest—such as climate change and the loss of undiscovered medicines.

Environmental organizations also try to educate governments, international organizations, and large businesses on the harmful effects of logging without planning to restore the resources they take. They educate these organizations of the benefits of sustainable forestry. Conservationists believe that through education, the decision makers of governments and businesses will see the benefit of preserving forest resources and will make future decisions not to cut them down.

Every person can play a significant role in conserving forest resources. For example, instead of using rain forest wood to build houses and furniture, using recycled wood or using wood grown on tree farms is more environmentally responsible. Reducing the demand for beef from ranches in tropical forests can help deter deforestation and erosion. Controlling pollution will also help the health and future of the rain forests.

Many environmental organizations have been successful over the years convincing governments to change the laws that will protect the rain forests. Some organizations, such as the Rainforest Alliance, offer ways that schools in the United States can "adopt" a rain forest by raising money to support the purchase and sustainable management of tropical forestlands. Donors can even choose which project they want to support.

Progress has been made toward conserving resources through establishing protected areas, such as parks and preserves. In some countries, it is against the law to cut down certain types of rare trees or collect rare plants. Unfortunately, today most of the world's rain forests remain unprotected.

According to the U.S. Department of Agriculture, other methods of conservation include the establishment of seed banks. Because future plants have the promise of new applications and uses—such as a source of new medicines, new sources of energy, new foods, and new environmental benefits—scientists keep a supply of seeds secure in seed banks.

Seed banks are used to store wild plants, cultivated plants, and sci-entifically developed plant varieties. The seeds can either be frozen in liquid nitrogen or stored in airtight containers. Seed banks are designed to constantly control the humidity, temperature, and pressure inside the bank. Seed banks store seeds for rare plants, and threatened and endangered plants for preservation. Seeds are also stored for future research. Only a small percentage of the world's plants have been tested for their potential medicinal values. Storing the seeds allows scientists to be able to study the plants in the future with new technology as it is developed. The future of the world's forests depends on the conservation work, education, and research done today.

CONCLUSION: THE FUTURE OF THE FORESTS

The immense value of forests has been presented throughout this book. A forest is much more than just a place where trees grow— it provides food and building materials for people, habitat for wildlife, helps moderate climate, supplies oxygen to the atmosphere, controls erosion, and produces plants that have medicinal benefit.

As the world population rapidly increases, more stress and demand is being placed on forested lands. The goals of this chapter are to look at the issues important to the future and the solutions to pressing concerns. It focuses on what the future holds for temperate, boreal, and tropical forests; as well as the important roles of education, recycling, reducing, and reusing products. It then addresses what is in store for the next 30 years.

HOPE FOR THE FUTURE

Some scientists predict that by the twenty-second century, there could be twice as many people living on Earth as there are now. The implications of this raise many important questions. Where will everyone live? Will there be enough food? What will happen to the forests? How much air pollution will there be? What about the greenhouse effect? Will the forests be able to provide enough oxygen? What will happen to the hundreds of plant and animal species that live in the rain forests? Will they become endangered or extinct? How many sources of medicines from rain forest plants will never be discovered before they are destroyed? These are all important questions that scientists, conservationists, and forest managers have to consider now—they cannot wait for the future to give these issues attention.

Because conservation of natural resources affects the entire world, these plans and policies need to be on a global scale in order to make a lasting difference for the future. Many countries around the world are becoming more environmentally conscious about reducing waste, recycling, controlling pollution, and focusing more on the benefits of renewable resources.

Today is the time to make these plans and begin working toward goals—especially in the areas that demand serious and rapid attention, such as the destruction of the rain forests, which contain the Earth's richest wildlife habitats. Every day, large areas of rain forest are lost to miners, ranchers, farmers, and loggers. Many professionals estimate that at the current rate of rain forest destruction, all rain forests may be gone in the next 50 years. If changes in thinking occur and governments and private industries choose to manage the land in a sustainable way, there is hope for the future—forests can remain one of the Earth's most renewable resources.

THE FUTURE OF TEMPERATE AND BOREAL FORESTS

The temperate forests are in the most densely populated parts of the world. If they are to survive, they must be managed in a sustainable way. This is possible if forests are managed with harvest-generation methods—when a tree is cut down, more are planted in its place. When new seedlings begin growing in areas where previous stands have been harvested, the resulting forest has a continuous canopy and trees of all ages in it. When disasters, such as wildfire, occur, it is important to reclaim land (re-seed it so that the natural habitat returns) before invasive species further degrade it. When most of the forest is left intact, habitat for wildlife is also left intact.

It is important in these forests to manage them with multiple uses in mind—not just using forests as a source of wood, but as wildlife habitat, recreational areas, aesthetic areas of beauty, watershed management, and wilderness. Today, it is generally recognized that most, if not all, nondestructive uses of forests are valid. In the national forests of the United States, decisions on how to manage and use the forestlands are made through a land-use planning process in which the general public has an opportunity for input and involvement.

Conservation organizations are also making a difference toward protection and care of forest resources. With this increasing interest in the welfare of forested lands, scientists feel there is a chance that much of the remaining temperate forests can be preserved. But a healthy future for these forests will require expanding conservation efforts. More people will need to get involved.

THE FUTURE OF THE RAIN FORESTS

The conservation issues of the past seem simple compared with those of today. In the twenty-first century, human societies are concerned with many issues—global warming, deforestation, species extinction, and rising expectations. Growing populations must be fed, clothed, and sheltered, and people everywhere want higher standards of living.

The future of the world's magnificent rain forests and the plants that live in them now hang in the balance. Rain forests are being lost at rapid rates—lost to farming, ranching, and plantations; the construction of oil and gas pipelines; mining; building roads; the establishment of industries; and logging. The encouraging aspect of all this, however, is that there is a great deal of interest in rain forests today. This growing awareness about the loss of the forest trees and plants places pressure on industry and governments and encourages sustainable use of these forests.

There are some governments, large companies, and individuals around the world—along with environmental groups—that are making huge efforts to save rain forests. School children living in or near the rain forests are becoming active in protecting and replanting the forests for their future, and many are also campaigning to save the forests so that diverse habitats will still exist when they grow up.

People now have a choice to buy products that come from well-managed areas of rain forest and refuse to buy products made from rare plants. These actions taken in the next decade will decide the fate of large areas of rain forest, and the fate of the precious trees and plants that live in them.

Many conservationists believe that traditional management practices for rain forest conservation will not be enough. Businesses and governments will have to change not only business practices but also the values of industrialized nations and decision makers in tropical countries. In addition, the mind-set of making quick profits will also have to be changed—unfortunately, a task much easier said than done.

Conservationists believe it will be critical in the next few years to control and certify that timber coming from rain forests comes from tree plantations, not wild rain forest areas. It is also important for developed countries to help poorer farmers in the rain forest countries by reducing their demand for cash crops from the rain forests and by contributing financial aid in order to take the stress off the farmers so they are not as likely to clear more rain forests for farming income.

Most experts also believe that the problems facing the rain forests today will simply go away by locking up forests in reserves. The forests, however, are too important to the local people for that to be a workable solution. There is no doubt that tropical forests will be cut. It is better for them to be cut in an ecologically sound manner than to be cleared for poor-quality farmland or wasted by poor harvest practices.

The only real long-term solutions are: (1) increasing the efficiency of agriculture on suitable farmland; (2) increasing the efficiency of forestry, such as utilizing plantations instead of harvesting the natural rain forests; and (3) establishing reserves to protect species diversity. Many forestry experts believe that we have only begun to tap the potential for wise use of tropical forests. Many uses have yet to be fully explored. We are only starting to learn the value of tropical forests for medicines, house and garden plants, food and fiber, tourism, and natural resource education.

There are things that everyone can do in order to help save the rain forests. Education can help save the rain forests. When people see the beauty and understand the importance of these forests, they will strive harder to protect them. Education is important for not only the people that are indigenous to the rain forest, but also to people in developed countries (like the United States) so that they understand the role they play in the loss of the rain forests (such as the demand for tropical hardwoods for furniture).

The Solution to Disappearing Rain Forests

The problem of, and the solution to, the destruction of the rain forest is largely economic. Governments need money to operate, inhabitants need money to feed their families, and companies need to make profits. The rain forest is being destroyed for the income and profits it yields. Because money has such a huge influence, many believe offering better economic incentives (than the logging and mining companies may offer) to governments and the people of the rain forest would encourage them to work toward sustaining the forests instead of depleting their resources.

Many organizations have demonstrated that if the medicinal plants, fruits, nuts, oils, and other resources like rubber, chocolate, and chicle (used to make chewing gum) are harvested sustainably, rain forest land has much more economic value both today and in the long-term than if it is used to harvest timber, graze cattle, or is cleared for farming operations. These sustainable resources—not the trees—are the true wealth of the rain forests.

Rehabilitation, restoration, and protection of the rain forests are important steps toward ensuring their future. Some areas can be replanted, and others can be converted to improved forms of efficient agriculture to feed the local people so that they do not have to cut down more rain forest. Parks preserve the land by keeping harmful activities, such as logging and hunting, out. Parks also help the economies of rain forest countries by providing tourism opportunities for visitors. Local people serve as tour guides, park caretakers, and a source of many beautiful arts and crafts that tourists like to buy.

Something everyone can do is to learn to live in ways that protect the environment, such as recycling paper, conserving water, and driving fuel-efficient cars. People can also help save the rain forests by only supporting businesses that strive to reduce their impact on the environment through recycling and energy conservation.

EDUCATION—UNLOCKING THE MYSTERIES

In the United States, foresters recognized the value of information about forests, and a branch of forestry research was established in the Forest Service in 1915. Early research was done primarily in support of reforestation efforts, but as forestry grew in size and complexity, so did the research.

Today, the USDA Forest Service has six regional experiment stations located in forest regions. Each experiment station has several field laboratories, and they specialize in issues related to their geographic environment. They also operate a nationwide center for research and development of new technology relating to wood—including tropical woods. Two laboratories are dedicated exclusively to tropical forest research—one in Puerto Rico and one in Hawaii.

Research is vital for modern forest management. Today's foresters require vast quantities of data and knowledge of ecology. They must understand not only the parts of ecosystems, but also how different parts of the environment interact. Scientific investigations are conducted in support of all kinds of forestry activities—forest insect and disease control, sustainability, wildlife habitat management, fire prevention and

Canopy bridges are used to traverse through the thick upper canopies of the rain forest, zones where only certain plants and animals live. These bridges, made of rope, can be more than a hundred feet (30 m) above the forest floor. This canopy walkway is at Taman Negara, Malaysia. *(Photo by Rhett Butler, Mongabay.com)*

control, range and watershed management, forest products utilization, forest survey, reforestation, ecology, and economics. Fortunately, with this vast increase in data, GIS systems are able to assist forest researchers in determining the proper course of action for the future.

Education and research play a big role in halting the destruction of forests. There is a need for more research into identifying species (before they become extinct) and other services that forests provide, apart from timber. These include medicinal drugs, biological control of pests and diseases, soil generation, and climate control. Often, when a medicinal product is developed initially from a rain forest plant, laboratories are able to break down the chemical compounds and reproduce the drug synthetically in a laboratory, instead of depleting the actual source plant.

Education plays a critical role in the future of forests. As people become more aware of forest resources and how they can specifically benefit from them, they will begin to relate to the problem on a more personal basis and commit to being an active part of the solution.

RECYCLING, REDUCING, AND REUSING

Having to produce new materials from the land's resources takes a lot of energy and also causes impact in some way to the land that the resource is removed from. The land can stay much healthier if people recycle, reduce, and reuse products. Every American throws away about 1,000 pounds (454 kg) of trash a year. Everyone can take an active role in reducing, reusing, and recycling materials. In order to reduce consumption, each person should buy only what they need. Purchasing fewer goods means less to throw away. It also results in fewer goods being produced and less energy being used in the manufacturing process.

Products that can be used repeatedly should be bought. If items are bought that can be reused, rather than disposable items that are used once and thrown away, it will save natural resources. It will also save the energy used to make them and reduce the amount of landfill space needed to contain the waste.

Recycling should be a priority. Using recycled material almost always consumes less energy than using new materials. Recycling reduces energy needs for mining, refining, and many other manufacturing processes. Recycling a pound of steel saves enough energy to light a 60-watt light bulb for 26 hours. Recycling a ton of glass saves the equivalent of 9 gallons (34 L) of fuel oil. Recycling aluminum cans saves 95% of the energy required to produce aluminum from bauxite. Recycling paper cuts energy usage in half.

Efficiency and conservation are key components of *sustainability*—the concept that every generation should meet its needs without compromising the needs of future generations. Sustainability focuses on long-term strategies and policies that ensure adequate resources to meet today's needs, as well as tomorrow's. Every person can take an active role to help reduce waste at home by learning basic waste-saving habits. If every person took part in a conservation effort, large quantities of forest resources could be protected and saved for future generations.

THE NEXT 30 YEARS

The United Nation's Environment Programme (UNEP), as a result of conducting global environmental assessments, has expressed concern that many of the Earth's ecosystems have already been, and continue to be, impacted to the point of collapse. UNEP attributes much of this impact to massive worldwide overdevelopment, poorly planned development, overuse of freshwater resources, and worldwide pollution from human populations now and in the near future. They believe that even though positive action has been taken by North America and Europe to clean up the environment and by the international community to reduce the production and consumption of ozone-destroying chlorofluorocarbons (CFCs), declining world environmental quality and global warming threatens to overwhelm those successes.

Another finding by UNEP is that nearly 15% of the Earth's farmland has now been severely degraded through overgrazing, overlogging,

The natural beauty of the forest is an intangible benefit that is hard to put a value on, such as this artistic display of nature in the rain forests of Hawaii. If forests are not conserved, beautiful natural resources may be lost forever. *(Photo courtesy Nature's Images)*

overfarming, and chemical contamination. UNEP has also determined that 50% of the world's rivers are now seriously depleted or polluted. In addition, dams and other engineered structures have fragmented 60% of the world's largest 227 rivers and have, in turn, destroyed wetlands and other ecosystems that people depend on.

Whatever the findings of investigations like this, one thing is clear: conservation of the forests' precious resources is critical now—and in the future—if societies expect to maintain the standards of living they enjoy today. Forests present some of the world's most beautiful scenery and have some of the highest aesthetic values for everyone to enjoy. The fate of the world's forests can be reversed with the help of concerned individuals. The world's forests can continue to be one of the Earth's most beautiful, valuable, and renewable natural resources. All it takes is time, dedication, commitment, and working together for a better tomorrow.

Geologic Time Scale

Geologic period	Approximate years	Climate	Predominant life-forms
Precambrian	4,600–570 million years ago	Wet	First one-celled and multi-celled organisms
Cambrian	570–505 million years ago	Wet	First shells, trilobites dominant
Ordovician	505–438 million years ago	Wet	First fish
Silurian	438–408 million years ago	Swampy	First land plant fossils
Devonian	408–362 million years ago	Swampy	First amphibians
Carboniferous	362–290 million years ago	Swampy	Giant horsetails, ferns, club mosses, large primitive trees, giant amphibians, and dragonflies
Permian	290–245 million years ago	Cooler	Conifers, gingkoes, and other primitive plants
Triassic	245–208 million years ago	Drier	Cycads and meat-eating dinosaurs
Jurassic	208–145 million years ago	Cooler and wetter	Swamp cypress, ferns, longneck dinosaurs, and flying reptiles
Cretaceous	145–65 million years ago	Drier	Horned dinosaurs, snakes, and flowering plants—bulrushes and willow trees
Tertiary	65–2 million years ago	Drier	Earliest large mammals; extinction of dinosaurs (at the Cretaceous-Tertiary boundary 65 million years ago)
Quaternary	0–2 million years ago	Drier	Appearance of humans

NATIONAL FORESTS OF THE UNITED STATES

Alabama:
Conecuh
Talladega
Tuskegee
William B. Bankhead

Alaska:
Chugach
Tongass

Arizona:
Apache-Sitgreaves
Coconino
Kaibab
Prescott
Tonto

Arkansas:
Quachita
Ozark-St. Francis

California:
Angeles
Cleveland
Eldorado
Inyo
Klamath
Lake Tahoe
Lassen
Los Padres
Mendocino
Modoc
Plumas
San Bernardino

Sequoia
Shasta-Trinity
Sierra
Six Rivers
Stanislaus
Tahoe

Colorado:
Arapaho
Comanche
Grand Mesa
Gunnison
Pawnee
Pike
Rio Grande
Roosevelt
Routt
San Isabel
San Juan
Uncompahgre
White River

Florida:
Oconee
Chattahoochee

Idaho:
Boise
Caribou
Challis
Clearwater
Curlew
Coeur d'Alene
Kaniksu

St. Joe
Nez Perce
Payette
Salmon
Sawtooth
Targhee

Illinois:
Midewin
Shawnee

Indiana:
Hoosier

Kansas:
Cimarron

Kentucky:
Daniel Boone
Land Between the Lakes

Louisiana:
Kisatchie

Maine:
White Mountain

Michigan:
Hiawatha
Huron-Manistee
Ottawa

Minnesota:
Chippewa
Superior

Mississippi:
Bienville
Delta
Desoto
Holly Springs
Homochitto
Tombigbee

Missouri:
Mark Twain

Montana:
Beaverhead
Bitterroot
Custer
Deerlodge
Flathead
Gallatin
Helena
Kootenai
Lewis and Clark
Lolo

Nebraska:
Nebraska
Oglala
Samuel R. McKelvie

Nevada:
Humboldt
Toiyabe

New Hampshire:
White Mountain

New Mexico:
Carson
Cibola
Gila
Kiowa
Lincoln
Rita Blanca
Santa Fe

New York:
Finger Lakes

North Carolina:
Croatan
Nantahala
Pisgah
Uwharrie

North Dakota:
Dakota Prairie

Ohio:
Wayne

Oklahoma:
Black Kettle & McClellan Creek
Quachita

Oregon:
Crooked River
Deschutes
Fremont
Malheur
Mount Hood
Ochoco

Rogue River
Siskiyou
Siuslaw
Umatilla
Umpqua
Wallowa-Whitman
Willamette
Winema

Pennsylvania:
Allegheny

Puerto Rico:
Caribbean

South Carolina:
Francis Marion-Sumter

South Dakota:
Black Hills
Buffalo Gap
Dakota Prairie
Fort Pierre

Tennessee:
Cherokee
Land Between the Lakes

Texas:
Angelina
Davy Crockett
Sabine
Sam Houston
Caddo/LBJ

Utah:
Ashley
Dixie
Fishlake
Manti-LaSal
Uinta
Wasatch-Cache

Vermont:
Green Mountain
Virginia
George Washington
Jefferson

Washington:
Colville
Gifford Pinchot
Mount Baker-Snoqualmie

Okanogan
Olympic
Wenatchee

West Virginia:
Monongahela

Wisconsin:
Chequamegon
Nicolet

Wyoming:
Bighorn
Bridger-Teton
Medicine Bow
Shoshone
Thunder Basin

CONSERVATION ORGANIZATIONS

The following organizations are currently involved in forest conservation and management. Many of them offer interested people opportunities to become involved in conservation projects and forest education.

Action for Nature

www.actionfornature.org
Encourages young people to take personal action to make this world a
    better place for humans and nature.

Amazon Conservation Association

www.amazonconservation.org
To conserve biodiversity through development of new scientific under-
    standing, sustainable resource management, and rational land-use
    policy for Amazonian ecosystems.

The Amazon Conservation Team

www.ethnobotany.org

Pioneers new conservation strategies by combining indigenous knowledge with Western science to understand, document, and preserve the biological and cultural diversity of the Amazon.

Biodiversity Support Program

www.worldwildlife.org/bsp/

Promotes biodiversity conservation in many of the world's most biologically diverse areas; provides publications that represent the accumulated knowledge, lessons, and tools from more than a decade of work.

Canadian Parks and Wilderness Society

www.cpaws.org

Dedicated to wilderness protection of lands, plants, and wildlife throughout Canada. Offers volunteer opportunities in various conservation projects.

Center for Biological Diversity

http://biologicaldiversity.org/swcbd/

Protects endangered species and wild places of western North America and the Pacific through science, policy, education, and environmental law.

Center for Plant Conservation

www.centerforplantconservation.org

Dedicated to conserving and restoring the rare native plants of the United States, to save them from extinction.

Conservation Biology Institute

www.consbio.org

Helps save the diversity of life on this planet in two primary ways: applied conservation research and education.

Conservation International

www.conservation.org

Seeks to conserve the Earth's living natural heritage, our global biodiversity, and to demonstrate that human societies are able to live harmoniously with nature.

Earth Island Institute: Get Involved

www.earthisland.org/getinvolved/getinvolved.cfm

Strives to conserve, preserve, and restore this fragile planet.

Ecological Society of America

www.esa.org

Promotes ecological science by improving communication, raising public awareness, and increasing resources for science; seeks the appropriate use of ecological science in environmental decision making.

Endangered Earth

www.endangeredearth.com

A global source of information about the Earth's endangered animals.

Endangered Species Coalition

www.stopextinction.org

Supports stronger protection for our nation's imperiled wildlife, representing the millions of Americans dedicated to a strong Endangered Species Act.

Endangered Species Program

www.fws.gov/endangered

Information on threatened and endangered species in the United States from the U.S. Fish and Wildlife Service.

The Endangered Wildlife Trust

www.ewt.org.za/home.aspx

Works to conserve the biodiversity of plant and animal species in southern Africa.

Environmental Tipping Points

www.ecotippingpoints.org

Tells stores of people and nature.

Forests—Greenpeace U.S.A.

www.greenpeace.org/usa/campaigns/forests/

The forests campaign of the independent campaign organization that
uses nonviolent, creative confrontation to expose global environmental problems.

Friends of Ecological Reserves

www.ecoreserves.bc.ca

Raises awareness, provides information, and supports ecoreserves—permanent sanctuaries to preserve natural ecosystems and rare and
endangered plant and animal species—in British Columbia, Canada.

Indian Wildlife Club

www.indianwildlifeclub.com/mainsite/

Showcases Indian wildlife and nature through the National Parks of
India and other natural wonders, spreading the message of conservation and environmental education.

Journey Into Amazonia

www.pbs.org/journeyintoamazonia/

A well-designed overview covering the region's flora and fauna—
the life in the forest canopy, the waterways, and other aspects
of the Amazon rain forest; this PBS Web site also includes
teaching resources.

Madagascar Wildlife Conservation

www.mwc-info.net/en/

Seeks to protect animal and plant species and to enable a sustainable
future for generations for Madagascar's humans, animals,
and plants.

Mongabay

www.mongabay.com

To increase awareness of ecosystems and environmental stewardship.

The Nature Conservancy

http://nature.org

Its mission is to preserve plants, animals, and natural communities
that represent the diversity of life on Earth by protecting the
lands and waters they need to survive, including through
land purchases.

Operation Migration

www.operationmigration.org

Dedicated to the restoration of migration routes for endangered or
threatened species of birds.

Organization for Tropical Studies

www.ots.duke.edu

Provides leadership in education, research, and the responsible use of
natural resources in the tropics.

The Peregrine Fund

www.peregrinefund.org

Works to conserve birds of prey in nature.

Plant Conservation Alliance

www.nps.gov/plants/

A consortium of federal agencies and cooperators that seek to protect
native plants by ensuring that native plant populations and their communities are maintained, enhanced, and restored.

Primate Conservation Inc.

www.primate.org

Dedicated to studying, preserving, and maintaining the habitats of the
least known and most endangered primates in the world.

Rainforest Action Network—Action Center

www.ran.org/action/

Provides opportunities to help protect rain forests, including
writing letters, distributing information, and contacting
decision makers.

Rainforest Alliance

www.rainforest-alliance.org

Seeks to protect ecosystems and the people and wildlife that
depend on them by transforming land-use practices, business
practices, and consumer behavior; specializes in certifying
tropical products.

Rainforest Conservation Fund

www.rainforestconservation.org

Dedicated to preserving the world's tropical forests; the main project
is the Reserva Comunal Tamshiyacu—Tahuayo (RCTT) in the
Peruvian Amazon.

Rainforest Heroes

http://rainforestheroes.com/kidscorner/

Information from Rainforest Action Network regarding what kids can
do to save rain forests.

Rainforest Information

www.rainforrestinfo.org.au/background/welcome.htm

Background and educational materials that provide an excellent
overview to rain forest conservation from the Rainforest
Information Center.

Smithsonian Tropical Research Institute

www.stri.org

Seeks to increase understanding of the past, present, and future of tropical biodiversity and its relevance to human welfare.

Society of Conservation Biology

www.conbio.org

An international professional organization dedicated to promoting the scientific study of the phenomena that affect the maintenance, loss, and restoration of biological diversity.

Student Guide to Tropical Forest Conservation

www.fs.fed.us/global/Izone/student/tropical.htm

A program of the USDA Forest Service International Programs that promotes sustainable forest management and biodiversity conservation internationally.

Tropical Forest Foundation

www.tropicalforestfoundation.org

Promotes sustainable tropical forest management by gathering and disseminating information about its benefits and by demonstrating and teaching proper management practices.

USDA Forest Service

www.fs.fed.us

Provides maps and brochures, research and development, forest safety, as well as a fun and educational Web site for students to enjoy.

Wild Madagascar

www.wildmadagascar.org

Wildmadagascar.com seeks to raise interest in and appreciation of wild lands and wildlife, while examining the impact of emerging local and global trends in technology, economics, and finance on conservation and development.

World Rainforest Movement

www.wrm.org/uy/

An international network of citizens' groups working to defend the world's rain forests, including publication of a regular rain forest bulletin.

World Wildlife Fund

www.wwf.org

The WWF is involved in conservation and education projects around
the world. They also work with government policy makers to promote
responsible land stewardship.

abscission layer   A layer of cells across the base of a leaf stem; when this layer dehydrates and wind blows, the leaf falls from the tree.

acid rain   A general term for precipitation that has been acidified by pollution in the air.

adaptation   A behavior or body structure that makes an organism more successful in its habitat.

algae   Plantlike living things that mostly live in water.

alpine   Pertaining to or inhabiting mountains.

amphibian   An animal that lives both on land and in the water.

annual   A plant that lives for only one growing season.

arthropods   Animals that have a segmented body, jointed legs, and a hard casing on the outside of their bodies instead of bones; some examples are insects, spiders, and centipedes.

association   A plant community characterized by its dominant tree types.

biennial   A plant that lives for two growing seasons.

biodiversity   The variety of life in a certain location.

biomass   The total weight of all living plants and animals in a given area.

biome   An area that has a certain kind of climate and a certain kind of community of plants and animals.

bog   A patch of spongy, soggy ground.

boreal forests   Forests located in colder, northern regions.

broadleaf   A type of tree that has broad, flat leaves. Most broadleaf trees are deciduous.

buttress   The name for the roots that grow from the trunk of a tree above ground and help to support it.

camouflage   Colors and patterns that help an animal to blend in with its surroundings.

canopy   The main top layer of a forest; the canopy can rise as tall as 200 feet (60 m) above the forest floor.

carbon dioxide One of the main greenhouse gases found in the atmosphere.

cash crops Products such as cotton and sugar, which are sold as a way of earning an income.

cavity-nesting animals Animals that live in holes in snags or live trees.

chlorophyll The green chemical in plants that helps change water and carbon dioxide into energy for the plant.

classify In science, to group living things with other living things that share important characteristics.

clear-cutting Cutting all the trees from an area of land.

climax The plants and animals in a given community that will persist in that community as long as conditions remain stable.

conifer A tree that has needles and produces its seeds in cones; most conifers are evergreen; some common conifers are pines, firs, spruces, hemlocks, and cedars.

coniferous forest A forest in which most of the trees are conifers.

conservation The maintenance of environmental quality and resources.

control A miniexperiment that you do to make sure the data from the main experiment are correct.

deciduous Plants that drop all their leaves each year.

decomposers Organisms that break down plant and animal matter into simple nutrients that can be used again by plants.

decomposition To rot or break down into smaller parts.

deforestation The destruction of forests trees and plants.

dispersal The process by which young animals leave the nests in which they were born to find their own home range.

dominant species The species of plant or animal that is the most common in an ecosystem or the species that has the most influence on the ecosystem.

dry tropical forest   A tropical forest with a dry season and a rainy season.

ecosystem   A community of plants and animals, along with their nonliving environment.

ecotone   A border between two biomes, where the plants and animals of those biomes mingle.

emergent layer   The layer of extra-tall trees that poke out above the canopy in a tropical forest; some trees in this layer are as tall as a 15-story building.

endangered   In danger of becoming extinct.

entomologist   A scientist who studies insects.

ephemerals   Plants that sprout, grow, flower, set seed, and die back quickly.

epiphytic plants   Plants that grow on other plants.

equator   An imaginary line that divides north and south on the globe.

evaporate   To change from a liquid to a gas.

evergreen   Plants that keep their leaves through more than one year.

foliage   The leaves of plants and trees.

food chains   The transfer of food energy from producer (plant) to consumer (animal) to decomposer (insect, fungus, etc.).

forest management   The selective manipulation of vegetation to protect the forest resource and improve the quantity and quality of benefits derived from the forest.

fragmentation   The division of a large portion of the forest into smaller pieces.

fungi   Plantlike organisms that get nutrients by helping other plants decompose.

germination   The development of a seed into a seedling.

global warming   A change in the composition of gases in the air that causes the gradual warming of the Earth's surface.

gondola   A small metal cage that hangs from the arm of a crane.

greenhouse gases   Gases that act like a one-way barrier, allowing more of the sun's heat to reach Earth than is allowed to escape back into space; the trapped heat warms the atmosphere of Earth.

ground layer   The bottom layer of a tropical forest; herbs, ferns, and other small plants grow there.

gymnosperms   Plants that have unprotected or naked seeds, such as conifers and gingkos.

habitat   The place where a plant or an animal normally lives and grows.

hardening   A process by which a plant changes its internal chemistry in order to avoid frost damage during winter.

hardwoods   Trees that have leaves and produce their seeds in flowers; most hardwoods are deciduous; some common hardwoods are maple, oak, beech, and hickory.

herb   A soft plant that has no woody stems and whose green foliage dies all the way down to the ground each autumn.

hibernate   To enter a winter state of inactivity that involves a substantial drop in body temperature.

humidity   The amount of water vapor in the air at a certain temperature, as compared to how much water vapor the air can hold at that temperature.

humus   A layer of well-decomposed plant and animal matter.

intermediate forest   A forest that will be replaced by a mature forest.

intolerant   Unable to live under a certain specified condition, such as shading, flooding, or drought.

jungle   Dense undergrowth found in tropical forests where sunlight reaches the ground.

liana   A type of plant with a woody stem that clings to other plants.

lichen   An alga growing inside a fungus.

litter The natural debris, including needles, leaves, and twigs, that falls to the forest floor.

logger A lumberjack; a person whose work is logging.

lumber mill A sawmill that produces lumber.

marsh An area of wet, low-lying land near a pond or lake.

mesophytic Having a moderate amount of water in the environment.

microclimate The local climate of a small site, which may vary from the area's general climate.

midstory Bushes and small trees growing under the forest canopy or overstory.

mixed wood forest A forest with softwood and hardwood trees.

mycorrhizal fungi Fungi that grow in plants' root tips and help the roots to absorb water and nutrients from the soil.

natural resource A material source of wealth that occurs in a natural state.

needle leaf A leaf from a conifer.

niche An environment in which an organism could successfully survive and reproduce in the absence of competition.

nocturnal Active at night.

nurse log A fallen tree that has rotted enough for young trees to grow on top of it.

nutrients For plants, simple salts (nitrate, phosphate, potassium, sulfate, iron) necessary for life.

ovule The undeveloped seed of a plant found in its flower or cone.

parasite A plant or animal living in or on another animal or plant and deriving its nutrition from the host organism to the detriment of the host.

phloem A system of cells that carries food throughout a plant.

photosynthesis The process by which green plants use sunlight, carbon dioxide, and water to make their own food.

pioneer species   A plant or animal that begins a new cycle of life in a barren area.

plant biomass   The weight of all the plant matter—roots, shoots, stems, and other plant parts—for a given area.

pollination   The transfer of pollen grains, which are male, to the female parts (see *ovule*) of a flower or cone so that seeds may develop.

predator   An animal that hunts other animals for food.

prey   An animal that is eaten by another animal.

rain forest   A moist tropical forest that receives at least 80 inches (2 m) of rain each year.

renewable resources   Products such as fruit, nuts, and fish, which can be harvested regularly and will naturally make up their numbers.

reserves   Areas of land that are protected, usually because of the plants or animals they contain.

resilience   The ability of an ecosystem to maintain its functions through environmental changes.

resin   Sticky tree sap.

respiration   Energy-yielding oxidative reactions in living matter.

saprophytic plants   Plants that get all or part of their energy from decaying plant or animal matter, instead of from photosynthesis.

secondary forests   Forests that have regrown on logged or cleared land.

shifting cultivation   A practice by native forest people who clear and cultivate an area of forest and then move on before the land is exhausted, giving it time to recover.

shrub layer   The lowest part of a tropical forest from the ground to about 16 feet (5m) above the ground; the area includes woody shrubs that can grow with little sunlight.

snag   A standing dead tree.

softwood   Wood from coniferous trees.

species   A group of plants or animals able to mate with one another and give birth to young that can also mate with individuals of the group and give birth.

species diversity   The number of different kinds of plants and animals in a given place.

stratification   The levels of a forest, formed by trees, shrubs, herbs, and soil.

succession   The process by which a sequence of plant communities naturally replace one another in a given area.

taiga   A biome that is characterized by evergreen conifers such as spruce and fir and occurs north of the temperate deciduous forest.

Taxol   A chemical found in the Pacific yew tree that is valuable in treating cancer.

taxonomist   A scientist who is an expert in classifying living things.

temperate   Having a moderate climate.

temperate deciduous forest   A biome supporting broad-leaved trees that drop their leaves in fall.

threatened   Likely to become endangered in the future.

timber   Wood suitable for carpentry; also trees of the species, size, and shape necessary to produce such wood.

tolerant   Able to withstand shade, flooding, drought, and other environmental stress.

torpor   A sluggish condition that is not sleep or a hibernating state.

transpiration   The elimination of excess water through pores in plant tissues.

tropical forest   A forest near the equator in the part of the world known as the tropics.

tropical rain forest   Natural evergreen forest located in the tropics and characterized by high rainfall.

tropics   Areas that lie near Earth's equator.

understory layer   The layer in a tropical forest that is about 33 to 66 feet (10 to 20 m) above the ground; the understory layer contains young canopy trees, small palms, and adult understory trees.

woodland   Stand of trees thinner than a forest, with sparse enough rainfall that branches of neighboring trees do not usually touch.

xylem   A system of cells that carry water throughout a plant.

Banks, Martin. *Conserving Rain Forests.* Austin, Tex.: Steck-Vaughn, 1990.

Behler, Deborah A. *The Rain Forests of the Pacific Northwest.* New York: Benchmark Books, 2001.

Burnie, David. *Tree.* New York: Alfred A. Knopf, 1988.

Caufield, Catherine. *In the Rainforest.* Chicago: Chicago Press, 1984.

Chesire, Gerard. *Nature Unfolds: The Tropical Rainforest.* New York: Crabtree Publishing, 2001.

Chinery, Michael. *Secrets of the Rainforest.* New York: Cherrytree Publishing, 2001.

Clark, John, David Flint, Tony Hare, Keith Hare, and Clint Twist. *Encyclopedia of Our Earth.* New York: Aladdin Books, 1995.

Fitzsimmons, Cecilia. *Animal Habitats: Nature's Hidden Worlds.* Austin, Tex.: Raintree Steck-Vaughn, 1996.

Forsyth, A., and Ken Miyata. *Rain Forest Ecology—Central America.* New York: Scribner, 1984.

Fredericks, Anthony D. *Exploring the Rain Forest: Science Activities for Kids.* Golden, Colo.: Fulcrum Publishing, 1996.

Goodman, Billy. *The Rain Forest.* New York: Michael Friedman Publishing Group, 1991.

Graham, Kate. *Totally Amazing: Rain Forests.* New York: Golden Books Family Entertainment, 1998.

Green, Jen. *A Dead Log.* New York: Crabtree Publishing Company, 1999.

———. *Rain Forests.* Milwaukee, Wis.: Gareth Stevens Publishing, 1999.

Hall, Cally. *Closer Look at Forests.* Brookfield, Conn.: Copper Beech Books, 1999.

Haugen, Hayley Mitchell. *Life in a Forest.* Farmington Hills, Mich.: Thomson Gale, 2005.

Hickman, Pamela. *In the Woods.* Halifax, Nova Scotia: Formac Publishing, 1998.

———. *Tree.* Buffalo, N.Y.: Kids Can Press Ltd., 1999.

Huxley, Anthony. *Green Inheritance.* New York: Gasia Books, 1984.

Jukofshky, D., and Chris Wille. "They're Our Rainforests Too," *National Wildlife.* April/May 1993.

Kaplan, Elizabeth. *Temperate Forest.* Tarrytown, N.Y.: Benchmark Books, 1996.

Klum, Mattias, and Hans Odoo. *Exploring the Rain Forest.* New York, N.Y.: Sterling Publishing, 1997.

Knight, Tim. *Journey into the Rainforest.* New York: Oxford University Press, 2001.

Lasky, Kathryn. *The Most Beautiful Roof in the World: Exploring the Rainforest Canopy.* San Diego, Calif.: Harcourt Brace, 1997.

Lean, Geoffrey, Don Hinrichsen, and Adam Markham, eds. *Atlas of the Environment.* New York: Prentice Hall Press, 1990.

Lye, Keith. *Equatorial Climates.* Austin, Tex.: Raintree Steck-Vaughn, 1997.

Martin, Claude. *The Rainforest of West Africa.* Switzerland: Birkhauser Verlag, 1991.

McClung, Robert M. *Lost Wild America: The Story of Our Extinct and Vanishing Wildlife.* Hamden, Conn.: Linnet Books, 1993.

Miller, Chuck. *Scientists of the Biomes: Forest Scientists.* New York: Raintree Steck-Vaughn Publishing, 2002.

Pandell, Karen. *Journey through the Northern Rainforest.* New York: Dutton Children's Books, 1999.

Parker, Edward. *Forests for the Future.* Chatham, N.J.: Raintree Steck-Vaughn, 1998.

———. *Rain Forest Trees and Plants.* New York: Raintree Steck-Vaughn, 2003.

Patent, Dorothy Hinshaw. *Biodiversity.* New York: Clarion Books, 1996.

———. *Fire: Friend or Foe.* New York: Clarion Books, 1998.

Pringle, Laurence. *Fire in the Forest: A Cycle of Growth and Renewal.* New York: Simon & Schuster, 1995.

Rapp, Valerie. *Life in an Old Growth Forest.* Minneapolis, Minn.: Lerner Publications, 2003.

Ross, Kathy. *Crafts for Kids Who Are Wild About Rainforests.* Brookfield, Conn.: Millbrook Press, 1997.

Russo, Monica. *The Tree Almanac: A Year-Round Activity Guide.* New York: Sterling Publishing, 1993.

Save, Steven. *Animals of the Rain Forest.* Austin, Tex.: Raintree Steck-Vaughn, 1997.

Sayre, April Pulley. *Temperate Deciduous Forest.* New York: Twenty-First Century Books, 1994.

Scott, Michael. *Ecology.* New York: Oxford University Press, 1995.

Simon, Seymour. *Wildfires.* New York: Morrow Junior Books, 1996.

Staub, Frank. *America's Forests.* Minneapolis, Minn.: Carolrhoda Books, 1999.

Stille, Darlene R. *True Books Ecosystems: Tropical Rain Forests.* Danbury, Conn.: Children's Press, 2000.

Stone, Lynn M. *Temperate Forests.* Vero Beach, Fla.: Fourke Enterprises, 1989.

Taylor, Barbara. *Forest Life.* New York: Dorling Kindersley, 1993.

Westoby, Jack. *Introduction to World Forestry*. New York: Bassil Blackwell, 1989.

Whitman, Sylvia. *This Land Is Your Land: The American Conservation Movement.* Minneapolis, Minn.: Lerner Publications, 1994.

Woods, Mae. *People of the Rainforest.* Edina, Minn.: Abdo Publishing Company, 1999.

A

acidity, conifer needles and, 7
acid rain, 54, 80, 134
adaptations
  biodiversity and, 48
  competition and, 101
  conifers and, 7, 9
  forest development and, 20–22,
    67–70
  parrots, macaws and, 57
aesthetics, 93, 106–108, 163
Africa, 87
agriculture, 44–45, 73–74, 82, 94,
    157–163. See also tree plantations
agroforestry, 124, 126, 137–139
Alaska, 14
allspice, 96, 97
amber, 20
angiosperms, 19
animals, 23, 25, 58. See also wildlife
antelope, 114
aromatherapy, 103–104
atmosphere, 22, 60–61
awareness, importance of, 125, 156

B

Baka tribe, 45
bamboo, 100
bananas, 94, 95
bauxite, 87
belladonna, 103
bioaccumulation, 80
bio-based products, 123
biodiversity
  clear cutting and, 81
  defined, 3
  forests and, 54–57
  importance of to forest evolution,
    27–30
  as intangible good and service, 93
  loss of, 84–86
  rain forests and, 11–12
  temperate forests and, 11, 52–53
  tropical rain forests and, 29

uniqueness of forest life and, 46–58
value and importance of, 34–37,
    101–102
bioenergy, 123
biofuels, 123
biogeochemical cycles, 63
biological warfare, 101
biomass, 30, 123
biomes, 3–5
bioprospecting, 104–105
birds, 7, 14, 57–58, 96–97, 106, 141.
    See also specific birds
boreal forests, 5, 6–7, 98, 155–156
Brazil, 12, 74, 139
bromeliads, 48, 49
buffers, 42–43, 61
buttress roots, 49–50, 69

C

cacao trees, 54, 96
camouflage, 14, 67, 69
Canada, 7, 10
cancer, 36, 103. See also medicines
canopies, 5, 12, 14, 52–54, 160
carbon dioxide, 34, 60, 62, 86–87
Carboniferous period, 18, 21
carnivorous plants, 51, 56, 143
Cashinahau tribe, 45
cassava, 95–96, 97
Center for International Forest
    Research, 74, 139–140
certification programs, 123
charcoal, 74
chicle trees, 94
Chile, 14
chlorofluorocarbons (CFCs), 162
chlorophyll, 62
chocolate, 54, 96
clear cutting
  conservation and, 134, 140–141
  erosion and, 39
  impacts of, 29–30, 81–84
  management and, 111–112
climate, 2, 7–8, 10, 142

climate change
   adaptation and, 67, 70
   biodiversity and, 31
   conservation and, 134–135
   fires and, 78
   forests and, 61
   impacts of, 86–87
climax species, 26
cloud forests, 40, 41
competition, 3, 12, 38, 48, 68, 101
complexity, 59
computer modeling, 115–116, 126
coniferous forests, 9–10, 98
conifers, 6–7, 9–10, 21, 51
conservation
   campaigns for, 148–151
   disappearing species and, 142–143
   endangered plants and, 88, 141–142
   Endangered Species Act and, 143–144
   Forest Legacy Program (FLP) and, 127–128
   future of forests and, 156, 157–158
   individuals and, 151–153
   key issues for, 137–141
   necessity of, 131–134
   overview of, 130–132
   Smokey Bear and, 147–148
   TESS List and, 146–147
   threats to, 134–137
controlled burns, 78, 148
cottony seeds, 23, 24
Crete, 27
crown fires, 78
cultural resources, 44–46

D
David Suzuki Foundation, 15, 31
deciduous forests, 10–11
deciduous trees, 7
decomposers, 12–13, 15, 51
deforestation
   biodiversity loss and, 84–86
   climate change and, 86–87

   conservation and, 132
   erosion and, 74–76
   fire and, 76–80
   impacts of, 89–90
   logging and, 81–84
   mining and, 87
   nonrenewable resources and, 54
   parrots and, 57
   pollution and, 80–81
   rates of, 1
   tropical rain forests and, 28–29
   urbanization and, 72–74
detritus, 38–39, 43–44
developing countries, 72
development of forests
   adaptations and, 67–70
   biogeochemical cycles and, 63
   energy flow and, 31–62
   nutrient cycles and, 64–65
   overview of, 60–62
   tree growth and, 65–67
   water cycle and, 64–65
disappearing species, 142–143
diseases, adaptation and, 67
dispersal, 22–25
disturbances, succession and, 27
drugs. *See* medicines

E
ebony, 99
ecology, 3, 34, 58–59
economics, 35–37
ecosystems, 25–27, 34
ecotourism, 92, 106–108, 140
education, 125, 151–152, 158, 159–161
Efe Pygmies, 45
efficiency, 157–158
emergent layer, 12, 13, 14
endangered species, 115, 135, 141–147
Endangered Species Act, 135, 143–144
endemic species, 144–145
energy cycle, 34, 61–62
epiphytes, 15, 48–49
erosion, 39, 42, 74–76, 89, 111–112

evergreens, 6–7, 9–10, 21, 51
evolution of forests
   adaptations and, 20–22
   biodiversity and, 27–30
   human impacts and, 16, 27–30
   overview of, 16–20, 21
   seed dispersal and, 22–25
   succession and, 25–27
exchange pools, 64
extinctions, 18–19, 21, 84–86

F
fibers, 38, 99
fines, 144
fires. *See also* wildfires
   adaptation and, 67
   benefits of, 119–120
   conservation and, 129, 147–148
   impacts of, 76–80
   management and, 111, 114, 119–122
   old-growth forests and, 59
   Smokey Bear and, 147
food, 5, 36, 38, 66–67, 93–98
forest floor, defined, 52
Forest Legacy Program (FLP), 127–128
Forest Service, 112–115, 147–148
fragmentation, 81
fruits, 25, 36, 91, 96–97
fuel loading, 111
future of forests
   education and, 159–161
   overview of, 154–155, 162–164
   rain forests, 156–159
   recycling, reuse and, 161–162
   temperate and boreal, 155–156

G
Geographic Information System
   (GIS), 116–119
gliders, 23
goods and services. *See also* food
   bioprospecting and, 104–105
   drugs, 100–104
   overview of, 91–93

   tourism and aesthetic values and,
      106–108
   value of urban forests and, 105–106
   wood products, 98–100
grazing, 74, 162–163
Greece, 27–28
greenhouse gases, 31, 86–87, 134–135
groundwater, 11, 34–35, 38, 39–44.
     See also water cycle
growth rings, 66, 67
gums, 94, 98
gymnosperms, 18, 19

H
habitats
   Canadian boreal forests and, 7
   defined, 2
   extinctions and, 86
   fires and, 80
   forests and, 33
   fragmentation of, 81
   GIS mapping and, 117–118
   as intangible good and service, 93
   management and, 111
   snags as, 59
   tree plantations as, 141
hardwoods, 10, 84, 98, 127
harvest-generation methods, 155
hazard reduction, 114
herbal medicine, 103
herbivores, 61
hiking, 106–107
Hodgkin's disease, 102
humans, 16, 27–30, 44–46, 68
human waste disposal, 129, 150
humidity, 2, 39–40
humus, 37–38
hydrologic cycle, 34–35, 64–65

I
ice ages, 20
incentives, 123, 126–127, 140
indigenous people, 44–46, 101–102
individual management units, 125–126

individuals, 128–129, 151–153, 157
Indonesia, 92
insects, 51, 56, 67
intangible goods and services, 92–93
invasive species, 3, 58, 135, 143

J

Jurassic Park, 20, 40

K

Kalimantan, 56
kaolin, 87
kapok trees, 99
Kayapo tribe, 45, 46
Kenya, 73

L

Larsen, John E., 78
latex, 94, 99
"Leave No Trace", 143, 148–151
leaves, 15, 66–67
lianas, 50–51
lichens, 14, 49
livestock, 74, 82
logging, 15, 81–84, 140–141. *See also*
    deforestation
Long-Range Transboundary Air Pol-
    lution Agreement, 81

M

Madagascar, 48, 89, 102
mahogany, 141
Malaysia, 132–134, 160
management
    fire and, 76–78, 119–122
    geographic analysis and mapping
        and, 116–119
    individual efforts and, 128–129
    modeling, planning and, 115–116
    overview of, 109–112
    private landowners and, 127–128
    rain forests and, 125–127
    research and, 159–161
    sustainable forestry and, 122–125
    U.S. Forest Service and, 112–115

mapping, 116–119
Maroon tribe, 45
mass extinctions, 18–19, 21
medicines, 30, 31, 35–37, 86, 100–104
Mediterranean forests, 10
mining, 82, 87, 135–136
modeling, 115–116, 126
monocultures, 83–84
Mozambique, 73
multiple use management, 113, 156

N

National Cancer Institute, 36, 104–
    105
Natural Resources Conservation Ser-
    vice (NRCS), 42, 43, 137
niches, defined, 3
nitrogen, 42–43, 64–65
nonrenewable resources, 32–35, 37,
    54, 58
nutrient cycles, 38–39, 64–65
nutrients, 30, 51, 59
nuts, 94, 96–97

O

off-highway vehicles (OHVs), 88, 107,
    118, 136–137
oils, 97, 98, 99
old-growth forests, 59
Olympic National Park, 73
orchids, 48, 49, 51, 96
Organic Administration Act of 1897,
    112

P

Pangaea, 16–18
paper industry, 84, 137, 139
parrots, 55, 57, 135, 136
petroleum industry, 82
pharmaceuticals. *See* medicines
phosphorous, 64–65
photosynthesis, 2, 34, 62, 66–67
pioneer species, 26–27
pitcher plants, 51, 56, 143
planning, 115–116

plantations. *See* tree plantations
poaching, 135
poisons, 51, 56
pollination, 48, 69, 70
pollution
    conservation and, 134, 152
    greenhouse effect and, 86
    impacts of, 80–81
    nonrenewable resources and, 54
    research and, 113
    statistics on, 162–163
    streamside forests and, 42–43
population growth, 73–74, 123,
    154–155
precipitation, 2, 9–10, 39–40
predation, 3, 68
preserves, 151, 152
private landowners, 127–128
prospecting, 104–105
pygmies, 45

R
rafflesia, 53
rainfall, 2, 9–10, 39–40
Rainforest Alliance, 123, 125, 140, 152
rain forests
    bioprospecting in, 104–105
    food and, 93–94
    future of, 156–159
    grazing and, 74
    humans and, 28–29
    logging in, 84
    management and, 125–127
    overview of, 11–12
    soils and, 39
    statistics on, 30, 36, 132, 140
    succession in, 27
    temperate, 14–15
    temperate vs. tropical, 15
    tropical, 12–14, 22, 31
rare species, 142
real-time monitoring, 116, 118
recreation, 88, 93, 106–108, 129
recycling, 88, 137, 152, 161–162

redwood trees, 52, 81
remote sensing, 116, 118
renewable resources, 32–34, 59
research, 113, 114, 139–140, 159
resilience, 69
resins, 20, 98
restoration, 139
reuse, 137, 161–162
roads, 81–83
roots, 49–50, 64–65, 69
rubber, 99

S
sanitation, 129, 150
sapodilla trees, 94
saprophytes, 51
satellites, 116, 118
Saudi Arabia, 18
seed banks, 152–153
seeds, 22–25, 96–97. *See also*
    gymnosperms
selective logging, 83
sequoia trees, 4, 5, 51–52
serotinous, 25
services. *See* goods and services
shifting cultivation, 44–45, 73–74
shrub and herb layer, 52
slash-and-burn farming, 82, 84
Smokey Bear, 147–148
soils. *See also* erosion
    agriculture and, 73–74
    boreal forests and, 7
    buttress roots and, 49–50
    effect of on plant diversity, 2
    epiphytes and, 48
    nutrient cycles and, 65
    temperate deciduous forests and, 10
    tropical rain forests and, 12
    value and importance of, 37–39
Somalia, 73
spinners, 23, 24
subsidies, 126
succession, 25–27, 67
sunlight, 2, 61

supercontinents, 16–18
suppression of fire, 76–78, 120–122
sustainability, 162
sustainable forestry, 122–125, 126, 137
Suzuki, David, 15, 31

T

taiga, 5, 6–7, 98, 155–156
tangible goods and services, 92–93
Tanzania, 73
Taxol, 35, 103
teak, 141
temperate forests
    future of, 155–156
    ice ages and, 20
    latitude and, 5
    overview of, 7–11
    rain forests, 14–15
    urbanization and, 73
    water quality and, 40–42
    woods from, 98
temperatures, 2, 7, 11, 15
TESS List, 144, 146–147
thinning, 140–141
threatened species, 142–143
tourism, 92, 106–108, 140
traditional medicine, 102
transpiration, 33, 39–40, 62
tree plantations, 82–84, 124, 127,
    137–139, 141
tree rings, 66, 67
trees, 65–67, 88
tropical forests, 5, 11–15
tropical rain forests, 22, 31. *See also*
    rain forests
Tukano tribe, 45

U

understory, 12, 13, 52–54
United Nations Environment Pro-
    gramme (UNEP), 162–163
urban forests, value of, 105–106
urbanization, 72–74, 82, 135
U.S. Forest Service, 112–115, 147–148

V

vines, 50–51

W

Wasatch National Forest, 9, 107
water, 23, 25, 38, 39–44
water cycle, 34–35, 64–65
water quality, 74–75, 80–81, 135,
    163
waxes, 99–100
weather, 61, 67
Week's Law of 1911, 112
wilderness areas, 114, 126
wildfires, 23, 25. *See also* fires
wildlife. *See also* animals; endangered
    species
    Canadian boreal forests and, 7
    clear cutting and, 81–83
    conservation and, 129
    diversity of, 54–57
    erosion and, 74–75
    as nonrenewable resource, 58
    rain forests and, 11–12
    seasons and, 62
    seed dispersal and, 23, 25
    seeds and, 96–97
    shrub and herb layer and, 52
    temperate forests and, 11
    trees and, 141
    tropical rain forests and, 13
wind, 2, 23–24, 78, 80–81
wood, 98–100, 113. *See also* tree
    plantations
World Wildlife Fund, 125, 132

Y

Yanamamo tribe, 45
Yellowstone National Park, 76–78
Yukon Flats National Wildlife Refuge,
    133

Z

Zimbabwe, 139

ABOUT THE AUTHOR

JULIE KERR CASPER holds B.S., M.S., and Ph.D. degrees in earth science with an emphasis on natural resource conservation. She has worked for the United States Bureau of Land Management (BLM) for nearly 30 years and is primarily focused on practical issues concerning the promotion of a healthier, better-managed environment for both the short- and long-term. She has also had extensive experience teaching middle school and high school students over the past 20 years. She has taught classes, instructed workshops, given presentations, and led field trips and science application exercises. She is the author of several award-winning novels, articles, and stories.